The Smart Study

Louise Tamblin and Pat Ward

The Smart Study Guide

Psychological Techniques for Student Success

Blackwell
Publishing

BLACKWELL PUBLISHING
350 Main Street, Malden, MA 02148-5020, USA
9600 Garsington Road, Oxford OX4 2DQ, UK
550 Swanston Street, Carlton, Victoria 3053, Australia

First published 2006 by Blackwell Publishing Ltd

1   2006

Library of Congress Cataloging-in-Publication Data

Tamblin, Louise.
The smart study guide: psychological techniques for student success /
Louise Tamblin and Pat Ward.
p.   cm.
Includes bibliographical references and index.
ISBN-13: 978-1-4051-2117-0 (pbk. : alk. paper)
ISBN-10: 1-4051-2117-3 (pbk. : alk. paper)
1. Study skills.   2. Learning.   3. Multiple intelligences.
4. Cognitive styles.   5. Critical thinking.   I. Ward, Pat.   II. Title.

LB1049.T246 2006
371.3'0281—dc22
2005034216

A catalogue record for this title is available from the British Library.

Set in 9.75/14pt Bell Gothic
by Graphicraft Limited, Hong Kong
Printed and bound in Singapore
by COS Printers Pte Ltd

The publisher's policy is to use permanent paper from mills that operate a
sustainable forestry policy, and which has been manufactured from pulp processed
using acid-free and elementary chlorine-free practices. Furthermore, the publisher
ensures that the text paper and cover board used have met acceptable
environmental accreditation standards.

For further information on
Blackwell Publishing, visit our website:
www.blackwellpublishing.com

Contents

Finding Your Way Around ...

Listed below are the special features included in the book, and where to find them.

Danger! points

35, 48, 54, 55, 65, 70, 73, 80, 93, 96, 145, 155, 164, 178, 214, 227, 243, 246

Did You Know?

> **DID YOU KNOW THIS?**
>
> 'The presence of daylight in classrooms was significantly and positively associated with faster learning rates or higher test scores among a sample of 8,000 students from different climates and educational environments.'
>
> Heschon & Knecht 2002

17, 45

How Can I Use This Right Now in My Study? Q

47, 48, 50, 51, 53, 54, 70, 77, 78, 79, 95–6, 127–8, 207

Interesting Fact/Findings

INTERESTING FINDING

2, 88, 92, 96, 100, 102, 133, 136, 220

En

It Worked for Me

Looking Ahead (tips for the future)

Things to Think About

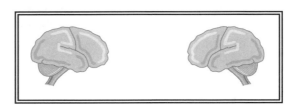

Top Tips

Try This (exercises/activities)

INTRODUCTION

Welcome to *The Smart Study Guide*. Since you're already looking through this book, we guess you have an interest in learning. We want to help you increase your repertoire of learning strategies, tools and techniques, in order to make your studying easier, more effective and more enjoyable. Does this surprise you?

Although we've all been to school and have many years' learning experience, typically our learning skills were gained through trial and error. Imagine what would happen if we learnt to drive without anyone to point out the brakes or explain the purpose of the clutch. Some people might stumble across them, some might learn by watching other drivers, and others might get by without ever changing gear! Do you think people's driving performance would be a good reflection of their potential? We don't!

And yet this is what happens with learning. The learning equivalents of a clutch or an accelerator *do* exist, and by using them appropriately you can learn more effortlessly and efficiently. Just as a skilled driver judges the correct pressure to apply to the accelerator or brake, so the skilled learner will know which learning techniques to use and when. We hope this book will help you to develop your learning skills, so your learning experiences will be easier, faster and more enjoyable.

1 Becoming an Effective Learner

KEY POINTS

☐ There is more pressure to learn than ever before
☐ Many students do not receive advice on how to learn
☐ It is good practice to consider how your personal circumstances may affect your learning
☐ Your current learning behaviours may not be the most effective
☐ There are tools and techniques available to help you become an effective and successful learner

THE LEARNING PARADOX

In this chapter we explore the learning paradox, and help you identify your personal learning profile and your current learning behaviours.

TRY THIS

At this point, ask yourself if you have ever received any advice on how to learn more effectively. Why was the advice given? How did you act on it? What was the outcome?

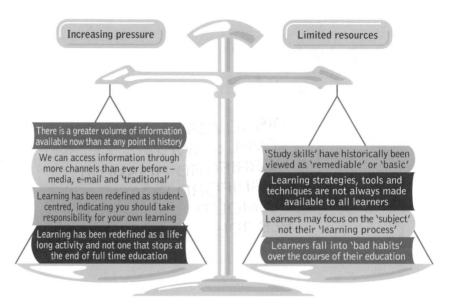

Figure 1.1 The learning paradox

The need for a considered approach to learning is more pressing than ever before. Figure 1.1 illustrates the paradox between the importance attached to learning versus the lack of knowledge about learning strategies and tools. Perhaps the biggest paradox is that students are often advised to 'do what works', without any guidance on how to identify what that means for them.

INTERESTING FINDING

The UK government is committed to increasing the number of undergraduates to 50 per cent of 18-year-old school leavers. Yet the UK non-completion rate for full-time students commencing in 2000–1 was 15 per cent and a greater proportion of mature students than younger discontinued (HEFCE 2003).

Table 1.1 Frequently expressed hopes and fears

I hope that	I fear that
• The course is interesting and stimulating • My learning will be useful for the future • I understand everything • The course will challenge me • The course is up to date • I will be successful/I will pass the exams/course • I will stay to the end • The tutors are helpful and knowledgeable • The other students are friendly and supportive • I can find enough time after work	• The course is too difficult • I will find it boring • I will be unsuccessful • There will be too much to do • I won't get on with tutors • I won't get on with the other students • I've made the wrong decision

HOPES AND FEARS

Most learners commence a new learning programme with a mix of hopes and fears. Table 1.1 (above) shows some that we've encountered in the past. Do you identify with any? Are there others that you want to include?

While you may share many of your hopes and fears with other students, your personal circumstances are unique to you. They provide the context within which learning will occur and so it is worth analysing how your own unique circumstances may affect your learning.

YOUR LEARNING PROFILE

At every point in your life there are likely to be personal circumstances that may facilitate, or impede, your learning progress. By identifying these factors you can then devise strategies to enhance or reduce them. The activity on the next page will help you to create your own learning profile.

TRY THIS

Take time to consider your current personal situation. The questions here are designed to help you do this, although feel free to add others that seem appropriate. Then, write your answers on to the blank mindmap opposite and consider the whole picture. What does your learning profile show? How can you enhance the aspects likely to assist learning and lessen those likely to hinder? Write your observations and intentions in the white boxes.

1. Why did I choose this course?
Subject interest?
My employer's decision?
I didn't know what else to do?
Parental pressure?
I followed friends?
Future career planning?

How might my reasons affect my learning?

2. What other time commitments do I have at present?
Family commitments?
Other study commitments?
Employment commitments?
Leisure/hobby commitments?

How can I best combine these commitments with my study?

3. Are there any potential barriers to effective learning?
Am I physically and mentally well?
Do I have recent study experience?
Is my partner/family supportive?
Financial issues?

To what extent will these barriers reduce my likelihood of success?

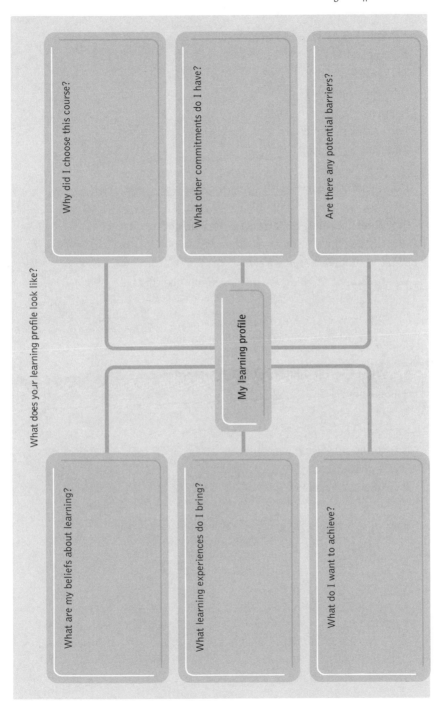

What does your learning profile look like?

Why did I choose this course?

What other commitments do I have?

Are there any potential barriers?

My learning profile

What are my beliefs about learning?

What learning experiences do I bring?

What do I want to achieve?

4. What do I want to achieve?
A qualification?
Top marks?
Parental approval?
Improved career prospects?
Personal fulfilment?
Time out of the office?

How might my goal(s) affect my motivation?

5. What learning experiences do I bring?
What have I previously studied?
What level have I studied at?
What mode of learning – attendance, on-line, distance, blended?
How successful was I?

What are the implications for this programme?

6. What are my beliefs about learning?
It is hard work?
It is enjoyable?
I am no good at it?
It requires self-discipline?
It is a chore?
It is time well spent?

How will such beliefs influence my learning behaviour?

LOOKING AHEAD

Any aspect of your profile can change over time. Our suggestion is to complete a learning profile at the beginning of each new programme of study, when it is always useful to evaluate 'where you are'. Similarly, you might review your profile during a longer programme of study, to see if your profile is still valid or whether there are new considerations.

TOP TIP

If you feel that your personal circumstances are working against you, try to share this with your tutor or programme leaders sooner rather than later. They may be able to help, by offering extensions on course work, or information on bursaries, for example. Battling on alone usually makes it harder to alleviate problems.

CURRENT LEARNING BEHAVIOURS

As an adult learner you bring many years of experience to any new learning programme. Some of the learning 'habits' collected along the way may be more constructive than others! We'll begin to appraise these habits here and explore them and others in the remaining chapters.

Now take a look at table 1.2 on page 8. To what extent do you agree with each statement?

How did you find these questions? Were they easy to answer? Have you ever thought about the issues before?

Let's consider what your answers mean and how this book might help you.

Table 1.2 Are you an effective learner?

	1 (strongly disagree)	2	3	4	5 (strongly agree)
I usually pass exams through last-minute cramming	☐	☐	☐	☐	☐
I look at all the recommended reading methodically and in depth	☐	☐	☐	☐	☐
By the end of a programme of study I have notebooks full of detailed notes	☐	☐	☐	☐	☐
My memory always seems to let me down	☐	☐	☐	☐	☐
I try to move on as soon as a topic is completed	☐	☐	☐	☐	☐
I find group work difficult – I never feel my voice is heard	☐	☐	☐	☐	☐
I use the same study skills that I used at school	☐	☐	☐	☐	☐
I like to play hard and work hard. Sometimes after a long study day, I'll party all night.	☐	☐	☐	☐	☐
I wish I could make my essays more original – I tend to regurgitate what I have read	☐	☐	☐	☐	☐
I sometimes become so engrossed in studying I don't move for hours	☐	☐	☐	☐	☐
People say 'play to your strengths' but I'm never certain what mine are!	☐	☐	☐	☐	☐
I find out about the best ways to learn	☐	☐	☐	☐	☐

'I usually pass exams through last minute cramming'

Did you agree strongly? Although this may have been an effective strategy in the past, you are likely to find that it does not guarantee success at more advanced levels of study. Few graduate level exams, for example, seek rote learning only. Instead, you are expected to show your knowledge *and* your understanding, and so you need to have thought through your stance on controversial theories or research before entering the examination room.

You may find it useful to read the section on planning your study (page 31), together with chapter 7, on how to remember information, and chapter 10, which explores how to evaluate information.

'I look at all the recommended reading methodically and in depth'

You may have thought 'agree strongly' was the desirable answer here, yet this is not the case. Many people believe that reading all the recommended reading is the sign of a conscientious student. Yet there is no need to work through an entire reading list once you know and understand the material. Not all reading needs to be in depth and the trick is to focus your efforts where they are needed most.

There is no need to read everything in the same way, and you can learn to adapt your reading strategy to fit your purpose. If you 'agreed' with this statement, take a look at chapter 6 (reading techniques).

'By the end of a programme of study I have notebooks full of detailed notes'

Well done if you strongly disagreed! Just as 'more' reading need not equal 'better', so the same applies to note-taking. The notes that you make should be clear and concise, rather than lengthy. This helps to avoid plagiarism and increases the likelihood that you will read through your notes in the future. See chapter 8 for more on effective note-taking.

'My memory always seems to let me down'

If you 'strongly disagree' you've probably already acquired a number of tools to help you remember effectively. But if this is an area that you struggle with, take a look at chapter 7. There you will see that memorisation involves focus, encoding and retrieval and there are many tools to make this process more efficient.

'I try to move on as soon as a topic is completed'

If you strongly agreed then our advice is to try slowing down and taking stock. Can you make links between the completed topic and those still to come? Making associations between topics should lead to additional understanding. And reflecting on the learning process itself (chapter 12) means you can adopt even more successful strategies for the future.

'I find group-work difficult – I never feel my voice is heard'

It can be difficult to make your voice heard in group-work. If you rated this statement 'strongly agree' then see chapter 5 (working with others) for hints on how to make group-work a success, both now as a learner and in the future. If you strongly disagreed you might also want to read the chapter to check that you are striking the right balance been listening and contributing.

'I use the same study skills that I used at school'

Schools tend to emphasise verbal and logical learning. Why not learn about a whole range of approaches and give yourself a chance to use different learning preferences? (See chapter 4, Learning Preferences.)

'I like to play hard and work hard. Sometimes after a long study day, I'll party all night'

If you rated this 'strongly agree' then don't worry! We are certainly not advocating ceaseless study; however, you do need a certain amount of sleep to consolidate your learning after a day of study. Why not take a look at the section on sleep (page 24).

'I wish I could make my essays more original – I tend to regurgitate what I have read'

We hope you rated this 'strongly disagree'. The best essays are not about regurgitation, they are about presenting an original argument in your own words.

If you showed more agreement then you might benefit from ideas on how to think about a topic in a new way or approach essay writing. Try chapters 9 and 10 for some hints and tips.

'I sometimes become so engrossed in studying I don't move for hours'

This sounds a wonderful state to be in – perhaps an example of flow (see page 29). But it's worth remembering your physical needs too, by making sure that you drink, eat and move! (See chapter 2.)

'People say "play to your strengths" but I'm never certain what mine are!'

Whether you agree or disagree it is work looking at chapter 3 on multiple intelligences, which provides the opportunity to look at yourself in new ways. Which of your intelligences are natural strengths? And where is there room for improvement?

'I find out about the best ways to learn'

Well, as you're reading this book, we suspect you 'agree' with this statement and hope you want to find out more!

The book is designed to help you dip into individual chapters in your preferred order. We hope you find it useful.

SUMMARY

We hope this chapter has whetted your appetite. The main points to remember are:

- Learners are not always well equipped to learn the masses of information available to them
- Your personal circumstances can also affect your learning effectiveness
- You may already have acquired some poor or counterproductive learning habits
- There are tools and techniques available to help you become an effective learner.

2 Preparing for Study

KEY POINTS

☐ Your environment affects how well you learn
☐ Physiological preferences and needs matter
☐ Be aware of and manage your mental state: Aim for 'Flow'!
☐ Follow a 'study plan'
☐ Watch out for displacement activities

INTRODUCTION

This chapter will help you ensure every study session is as effective as possible. We recommend your preparations address four distinct aspects: your environment, your body, your mind, and your study plan. Let's look at each of these in turn.

1 PREPARE YOUR ENVIRONMENT

Did you know that your physical environment affects your cognitive performance? (US Department of Ed. 2000, Yong & McIntyre 1992). While there probably isn't a great deal you can do to modify or improve your classroom or lecture theatre, you *can* take responsibility for your home study environment, so why not make it as effective as possible *for you*?

Follow a study plan

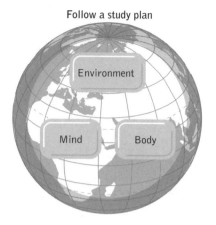

Figure 2.1 Preparing for study

IT WORKED FOR ME

'All through school, my parents and I argued constantly about my study habits. They insisted I couldn't be learning unless I was sitting at a desk, working in silence. I was never comfortable like this, and found it very difficult to concentrate. Now I know more about my own preferences, and the research around "best conditions", I take them into account and find I can concentrate better and for much longer periods. It's great.'

There are many different aspects to the environment, which have been shown to affect cognitive performance and test results. These include:

- temperature (Harner, 1974)
- light (Heschong & Knecht 2002)
- sound (Evans & Johnson 2000)
- aesthetics (Cheng 1994)
- design and formality (Nganwa-Bagumah & Mwamwenda 1991).

Where students have a strong preference, they perform significantly better in situations where their environmental preferences are met. (Hathaway 1988, Moore & Warner 1998.)

TRY THIS

Can you think of a time when you walked into a room and immediately felt inspired? What was it like? Jot down any specific details about the room or place that you can remember.

Can you think of a room or place that you couldn't 'escape' from quickly enough? How was this different from the inspirational room or place you've noted above?

Experiences like the ones you noted above are probably keying into some of your stronger environmental preferences . . . and you should take note of them. Among other things, they can help you improve your memory and thinking skills.

Take a few moments to complete column A in table 2.1 (page 16). Now, imagine you can design your own study area with an unlimited budget and no physical constraints. How would it differ from your current space? Make a note of your own 'perfect study place' in column B of table 2.1 and add your own notes about the research findings as you read through the rest of the chapter.

Let's look at each of these environmental and physical conditions in turn. As you work through the following sections, reflect on how well your current study environment a) meets your criteria for a 'perfect' study place and b) matches the ideal conditions revealed by research. Then use column C of table 2.1 to note any ideas you have for improving any aspects of your current area, or other study places you might like to use.

Daylight

Q.   What's the best kind of light for studying?

A.   Bright, diffused natural daylight is the best for learning. Avoid direct sunlight, as this can cause glare and adjusting to high contrast areas not in direct sunlight can result in visual discomfort (Heschong & Knecht 2002).

Table 2.1 Environmental and physical factors which affect learning

Environment	Considerations	A: My current study area	B: My preferences	C: Improvement I can make
1. Light	Bright, gloomy, soft accent lighting, fluorescent lights, natural light, candles			
2. Temperature	Warm, cool; stuffy or fresh air; window open/closed, heater on/off			
3. Sound	Silence, birdsong, background 'hum' of traffic, children, office noise, conversations			
4. Décor	Pleasant, inspiring or neglected			
5. Posture	Desk (large or small?), chair (hard or soft?), floor, bed, couch, bean bags			
6. Music	None, Mozart, instrumental tracks, relaxation CDs			
7. Workspace	Large, open space, or small, private corner. Organised or cluttered?			
8. Odours	Pleasant (flowers, perfume, food) Unpleasant (car fumes)			
9. Privacy	Constant flow of interruptions, or privacy			
10. Supplies	Information sources (textbooks, articles, notes, tapes), materials (paper, index cards, coloured pens)			

Physical	Considerations	A: My current behaviour	B: My preferences	C: Improvement I can make
11. Mobility	Sit still or move around			
12. Food & drink intake	Constant snacking and drinking Only eat and drink during study breaks			
13. Time of day/ Biorhythms/	Early morning, afternoon, late evenings Daily routine or no routine			
14. Sleep	Well rested or tired			

Q. *Does it matter how bright the light is?*

A. Yes. Higher illumination levels have been consistently shown to improve performance on visual tasks (Heschong & Knecht 2002).

Q. *Is daylight mentally stimulating?*

A. It looks that way. Researchers believe daylight may stimulate the production of seratonin, a neural transmitter which increases alertness (Kuller and Lindsten 1992).

Q. *Are there any other benefits to daylight?*

A. Yes. Daylight has positive effects across a whole range of human performances. A number of reports are available on the New Buildings Institute Website.

DID YOU KNOW THIS?

'The presence of daylight in classrooms was significantly and positively associated with faster learning rates or higher test scores among a sample of 8,000 students from different climates and educational environments.'

Heschon & Knecht 2002

Temperature

If you have spent any time in extreme temperature conditions, it may be no surprise to learn that our ability to perform mental tasks is affected by changes in temperature. (For a review of the literature, see Schnieder 2002.) The ideal temperature for optimum learning is between 68° and 74° Fahrenheit (20°–23°C) (Harner 1974). What steps can you take to keep the temperature of your study area within this range?

Sound: Does background noise matter?

Yes. Unwanted and excessive noise can reduce your performance on a range of cognitive tasks (for a thorough review, see Earthman 2002). There is some evidence to suggest that even low-level noise may have a detrimental effect.

In a study by Evans and Johnson (2000), 40 female clerical workers were randomly assigned to either a quiet open office or one with standard low-intensity office noise, which included background conversation. After three hours, the workers in the noisy office experienced significantly higher levels of stress (as measured by urinary epinephrine) and made significantly fewer attempts to solve an unsolvable puzzle . . . though interestingly, they did not report feeling stressed!

We know that elevated stress causes the brain to release excess levels of epinephrine – a chemical that triggers changes in the hippocampus, which is an area of the brain important to memory and learning.

While this is only a small study, and research is ongoing, it might be worth paying attention to the level of background noise, and minimise it when you can!

Décor

Several studies have shown a significant link between quality of décor and student performance. (For a comprehensive literature review, see US Department of Ed. 2000.) Think about how you can improve the décor where you study. Don't choose a desk with graffiti, or one in an area that badly needs redecorating.

'Decaying environmental conditions such as peeling paint, crumbling plaster, non functioning toilets, poor lighting, inadequate ventilation, and inoperative heating and cooling systems can affect the learning as well as the health and the morale of staff and students.'

US Department of Ed. 2000

Music: Will Mozart Make Me Smarter?

Have you heard that listening to Mozart makes you smarter? Well, in the original experiment, published in Nature in 1993, Rauscher et al. gave headsets to a group of students and then played either white noise, relaxation music or Mozart for 10 minutes. Following this, the students were given a series of spatial tasks, and when the tests were given with less than a 10-minute delay, the Mozart group significantly outperformed the other two groups! These results caused great excitement in the media, and sparked a flurry of similar experiments by other researchers.

However, opinions are divided on whether the so-called Mozart effect is real, as some of the subsequent studies failed to find any significant effects. (Bridgett & Cuevas 2000, Steele et al. 1999). Although experts don't yet know enough to understand exactly why, the contradictory findings suggest the 'Mozart effect' may be dependent on the specific procedures and tests involved. For example, in an experiment similar to Rauscher's, Wilson and Brown (1997) found an order effect: the group with the greatest improvement in test scores listened to silence first, followed by relaxing music, and finally, Mozart. The evidence of an order-specific effect does support the idea that the details of the procedure affect the outcome, and may help to explain the mixed evidence to date.

Caution! Be careful about drawing general conclusions from individual experiments!

However, there are many studies which do support and expand the original findings. For example, Cockerton et al. (1997) reported that students who listened to stress-reducing instrumental music increased their results on a general intelligence test. This experiment was 'a repeated and reversed' study design: Both the music and nonmusic groups were tested twice, and then the conditions were reversed, so that each group took the tests under both conditions. This type of experimental design is generally regarded as more robust than Rauscher's original design, and adds weight to the pro-Mozart camp.

In a more recent study, Parsons et al. (2001) found that exposure to any auditory rhythm, not just the music of Mozart, enhanced both visualisation and mental rotation, and more complex rhythmic sounds led to greater enhancement than very simple rhythmic sounds.

So what's the bottom line?

We think there is plenty of evidence to suggest that listening to certain types of background music will improve your performance on certain tasks . . . and there is lots of evidence that music has a powerful and very positive affect on many aspects of our lives, including emotional and physical health . . . and the long-term benefits of studying music or learning to play an instrument are well documented (Campbell 1997, Jensen 2000 & Rauscher 2002).

TRY THIS

As part of your study preparations, why not track down the following music?

☐ Mozart
☐ Baroque music e.g. Albinoni, Bach (Brandenberg Concertos), Handel (Water Music), Vivaldi (Four Seasons)
☐ Relaxation CDs (e.g. Waterfalls, Rain Forest, Ocean Sounds)

Although the evidence is still unfolding, try to select pieces which meet the following criteria:

☐ Orchestral not solo instruments or vocals
☐ Adagio or andante movements
☐ Major key rather than minor
☐ Complex rhythmic sounds

Posture

How do you prefer to sit (or lie) when you're studying? Is your chair suitable? Is your table at a good height? It is important to be comfortable while you study, but it is also worth trying to develop good posture habits. The authors are not aware of any research linking postural effects directly with learning, but the links between posture and physiology, and the consequences of repetitive strain injury (RSI) are well established. If you're interested in learning more about posture, the 'Alexander Technique' has a good reputation and is widely used by musicians and performing artists.

Workspace

Do you think better in a space that is neat and tidy, with uncluttered surfaces? Or do you prefer to work in a disorganised space, with piles of papers and books? Also consider whether you like open-plan spaces, or cosy nooks. Choose a workspace where you feel comfortable and creative.

Odours

Smells can be very powerful memory anchors, and can affect your mental state. Strong odours, even delicious food smells, can be very distracting. Try experimenting with scented candles or air fresheners.

Privacy

Constant interruptions can have a devastating impact on the effectiveness of your study time – so manage them well. If you work in a shared space, make sure your friends and colleagues know when you are studying, and ask them not to interrupt you. Perhaps put a sign on your door, or have some kind of signal at your desk so that other people know not to bother you. Turn your phone off, and don't log in to your online chat or instant messaging service.

Supplies

Finally, think about any information sources (textbooks, articles, notes, tapes) and materials (paper, index cards, coloured pens) you might need, and make sure you have them to hand before you settle down to study.

Did you make a note of all your ideas for improvement in column C of Table 2.1? If you like formal assessments, Price et al. (1991) offer an analysis for adults which includes environmental and physical preferences.

2 PREPARE YOUR BODY (MEETING YOUR PHYSICAL NEEDS)

Mobility

In chapter 4 we discuss how some people prefer to be still when they learn, and others prefer movement. Dunn et al. (1986) found that student's results on recognition and memory tasks improved significantly when their mobility preferences were met. If you have a preference for mobility, then make sure you find a place to study that allows you to move freely.

> If you like to move when you study, even a simple technique like pacing can help you improve your memory.

Food intake and performance

Some people like to 'snack' and drink while they are concentrating. Ballone and Czerniak (2001) cite evidence that matching dietary intake preferences improves performance on a range of cognitive tasks. In many libraries and study halls, eating and drinking is prohibited – so be aware of your own preference and choose a place that works for you.

There are lots of magazine articles about the importance of water and the risks of dehydration, and a frequent recommendation is that we need 8×8 fluid ounces of water a day. However, this is probably rather simplistic: a report by the Institute of Medicine (February 2004) sets general recommendations for total fluid intake at 2.7 litres (91 fl. oz) per day for women and 3.7 litres (125 fl. oz daily) litres per day for men. These requirements can be met through all fluid and food intakes, not just water, and the required amounts are higher with prolonged physical activity or heat exposure.

Time of day

We've known for over a century that our internal or circadian rhythms influence both physiology and cognition. Our body temperature fluctuates with these rhythms. Some people's temperatures peak before noon, some in the afternoon, and some in the evening, and these patterns frequently change with age. What is particularly interesting from our point of view is that recent studies have shown that students' comprehension of material and performance on tests are significantly better during their preferred time of day (Biggers 1980, Callan 1998, Klavas 1994, Carskadon et al. 1998, Holloway 1999).

While you may still have to attend lectures and practical sessions at set times, you can select study times which are in tune with your own circadian rhythms. Work with your body, not against it.

TRY THIS

If you're not sure about your internal body clock, why not keep a diary for a week, and note down how alert or tired you feel at different times of the day?

Sleep: What's it worth to you?

An interview with Dr M., a professional mnemonist:

Pat: It's a real pleasure to meet you at last, Dr M.

Dr M.: Pleasure's mine. What can I do for you and your readers?

Pat: Well, perhaps you could start by telling us how you prepare for your record-breaking memory feats.

Dr M.: Well, if it's an evening event, as most of them are, I always have a nap in the afternoon.

Pat: Now that's a surprise. I thought you would be busy rehearsing.

Dr M.: I need my brain in tip-top condition.

Pat: Hmmm. I'm wondering what would happen if I took a nap after a study session. Do you think that would help me to learn?

Dr M.:   Sara Mednick and her Harvard colleagues think so.[1] They found that a 60–90 minute nap improved learning.

Pat: I wish I'd known that a few years ago!

Dr M.:   Well, that's not all. I read something a few months ago that found it only takes an average of 18.25 hours without sleep, before there is a significant reduction in cognitive performance.[2]

Pat: You're kidding, right?

Dr M.:   No, I'm absolutely serious. As far as I'm aware, no-one else has tried to repeat the results yet, but if it turns out to be a real effect, it has quite strong implications for our sleep habits, doesn't it?

Pat: Yes. I'm beginning to wonder how much of my struggle at college was due to sleep deprivation!!

Dr M.:   Well, you need to keep a sensible perspective on the issue, but I do think sleep is way undervalued, at least in contemporary western culture.

Pat: That's fascinating. Is there anything else we should know?

Dr M.:   Oh, yeah. This guy, Stickgold, taught a bunch of people some visual discrimination tasks. He retested one group after they'd had a full night's sleep, and their scores showed a significant improvement. He retested another group, this time only three hours after the original test . . . and guess what? Their scores showed *no* improvement. In other words, they hadn't learned a thing.[3]

Pat: That's not what I would have expected at all. So, is it fair to say that sleeping helps you learn?

Dr M.:   Yes, isn't that great news? And, Stickgold kept a third group awake all night after the study session, then allowed them to sleep as much as they liked the following two nights . . . then retested them, and guess what? There was absolutely no change in their scores.

Pat: So, *not* learning wasn't just about being tired. What you're saying is that we need to sleep following study in order to consolidate our learning. Is that it?

---

[1]   Mednick et al. 2003

[2]   Van Dongen et al. 2003

[3]   Stickgold et al. 2000

Dr M.:   Well, it looks that way to me.

Pat: So how do you manage when you're travelling?

Dr M.:   It's very difficult. Missing a night's sleep reduces mental performance in a whole range of areas, not just memory.[4] So, I do whatever it takes to maximise sleep the night before a competition or exhibition event.

Pat: Makes me wonder about the value of the all-nighters I pulled before my final exams. . . . Mmmm.

Dr M.:   I wouldn't recommend it for anyone.

Pat: Well, it sounds like sleep is a key strategy for you. Can I ask how much of your success you attribute to sleep?

Dr M.:   (Laughs.) Well now, that would be telling!

---

[4]   Harrison & Young 1997, 1998, 1999, 2000

3 PREPARE YOUR MIND

Where's your 'Thinking Cap'?

As children, were you ever told to 'put on your thinking cap'? If so, we bet you understood intuitively that it was a metaphorical hat, which had something to do with feelings, focus and readiness to learn. We know that pre-school children are great at learning. They don't need to be told how to focus on something . . . have you watched a young child who is totally absorbed in what they are doing? That's the kind of mental focus which makes for great learning.

TRY THIS

How would you describe your current state right now? Rate yourself on a scale of 1–10 on the following factors:

Curiosity

1 = I know this – and don't want to hear anything else ☐
10 = Wow, I feel curious and excited about new ideas

Alertness

1 = I'm exhausted and can hardly stay awake ☐
10 = I feel fantastic and full of energy

Present (or focus)

1 = My mind is really elsewhere today ☐
10 = I'm fully focused on what we are here to do
I've put all other things out of my mind

Now, calculate your Learning State. Multiply your three 'CAP' numbers together, and you should have a number between 0 and 1,000. This number represents your current learning state.

Curiosity × Alertness × how 'Present' =

How close to 1,000 are you? Many people are surprised how low their final number is. While there is nothing at all scientific about the formula, it can serve as a useful reminder of just how inefficient it can be to study in a less than optimal mental state.

(This idea was modified from a classroom exercise used by Kimberley Hare from Kaïzen Training.)

Q.   *How can you improve your CAP score?*

A.   There are two main ways: physiology and focus. Let's have a closer look at these.

Improving your CAP score: Physiology

Using physiology is as easy as moving. You can stretch, walk around, sit up straight, make faces, put on some upbeat music and dance round the room, or take some really deep breaths. Doing any of these may help you feel more energetic, and probably more open to ideas. You'll be in a better learning state.

If you're hungry or thirsty or too hot, it may be hard to concentrate on anything other than your hunger or thirst or desire to cool down. You can often improve your learning state by taking care of your biological and physical needs.

Unfortunately, the most common strategy used in our culture is perhaps the least healthy one . . . introduce some toxic substance into your nervous system! The reason alcohol, cigarettes and other drugs are used so widely are that they do change your state very quickly, . . . but we advise against this for study purposes!!!

Improving your CAP score: Focus

Have you ever thought about the difference between excitement and fear?

If not, take a moment and think about one really scary event (perhaps a job interview, exam or formal presentation) and one exciting event (perhaps a first date). How would you describe your physical state during each of these experiences? Did you have:

- rapid heart beat
- sweaty hands
- butterflies in your stomach
- loss of appetite.

Did you notice any similarities in your physiology for both events? It seems to us that the difference between fear and excitement is one of interpretation . . . or focus.

And the good thing is that your focus is under your control. You can't always change a situation, but you can control what you think, and that affects how you feel about that situation.

'Whether you think you can
or
think you can't
. . . you're right.'
Henry Ford

TRY THIS

Take a few moments and try and remember the last time you were completely absorbed in an activity. It doesn't matter what type of activity – it could be reading, playing computer games, rock climbing or chess, but whatever it was, you were so engrossed by it that you probably 'lost track of time', and the outside world ceased to exist. People sometimes call these 'optimal experiences', or being in a 'flow' state. How would you describe that experience? Was it enjoyable?

Now, imagine if your work and study tasks could be more like these 'optimal' experiences – so interesting and inherently enjoyable that you become absolutely absorbed in the moment, and feel the deepest sense of satisfaction while engaged in the task. It is much more satisfying and effective to learn because a task is enjoyable as opposed to useful.

Q. *I hate studying. Is there any way I can make it more enjoyable?*

A. Well, Mihalyi Csikszentmihalyi has spent his life researching enjoyment and happiness, which he calls 'flow'. He believes we have the capacity to turn any activity into a flow activity. The key is to focus on an aspect of the task that appropriately matches the difficulty, or level of challenge, to your skill level. As illustrated in figure 2.2, too much challenge results in anxiety and stress, and too little leads to boredom.

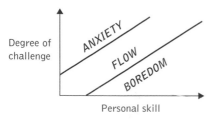

Figure 2.2 Achieving flow

According to Csikszentmihalyi (2002), you can transform any activity into a 'flow' one by following these five steps:

1 Set an overall goal, and as many sub-goals as are realistically feasible.
2 Find ways of measuring progress in terms of the goals chosen.
3 To maintain concentration, make finer and finer distinctions in the challenges involved in the activity.
4 Develop the skills necessary to interact with the opportunities available.
5 Keep raising the stakes if the activity becomes boring.
(Adapted from Csikszentmihalyi (2002), p. 97.)

Find the fun

So, let's take an example and see how this might work. Suppose you're studying anatomy and need to learn the names and location of all the bones, muscles and nerves in the body. If you look forward to memorising the information, this may seem like a natural 'flow' activity for you – and that's great. If not, what can you do to make task interesting and engaging, using the model above?

1. **Set a goal**: That's easy. You need to learn the names of all the bones, muscles and nerves in the human body, and their location.
2. **Find a way of measuring your progress**: How about turning it into a card game? You could use a pack of index cards, displaying the name for each bone, muscle or nerve, and the 'suit' or 'group' to which it belongs on the 'face' of each card. You can then invent a speed trial. For example, see how quickly you can locate all the cards for a particular group (e.g. facial nerves).
3. **Make fine distinctions in the challenge**: Here you need to introduce refinements to the original challenge. Why not time how long it takes to sequence the cards from the top of the skull down through the body to the toes? Or put the 'bone cards' in one deck, shuffle them, turn over the top card, and then sort through the other deck to find all the nerves and muscles which are attached to that bone. There are endless possibilities.

4. **Develop the skills necessary to interact with the opportunities available**: How easily can you devise different ways of testing yourself, either working alone or with a partner?
5. **Keep raising the stakes if the activity becomes boring**: For each activity, set yourself a target e.g. by Friday, I'll be able to pick out all the muscles and nerves which are attached to any five randomly selected bones within three minutes. And why not set yourself a reward for completing each challenge successfully?

If the idea of playing cards leaves you cold, perhaps you could challenge yourself to come up with a metaphor or visual image that captures the information you need to learn. So for example, if you need to remember the atomic number of the element Xenon, you could use the fact that the name, Xenon, comes from the Greek word meaning stranger. As it is a Noble gas, you might imagine a very noble-looking stranger (alien), perhaps with 54 eyes on long stalks coming out of his head to remind you that the atomic number is 54. You can sustain the challenge level by increasing the number of facts you include.

Now go back to the Thinking Cap exercise, and re-evaluate how you feel. 'Getting into flow' is about modifying your state by changing your focus.

4 FOLLOW A STUDY PLAN

With a clear focus on your 'big picture' goals, you can begin to design a study plan. There are lots of ways you can do this. We like the **abc** approach outlined below.

a) Study activities: Identify the different types

The first step is to identify all the different types of study activities that are involved in your course. We've shown some examples in figure 2.3 (overleaf). Can you think of any others?

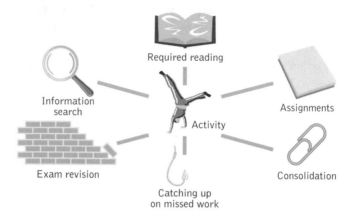

Figure 2.3   Types of study activities

b) Break down the tasks into sensible-sized chunks

The next step is to break down each activity into discrete tasks, with specific outcomes. For this, you need to decide:

* the best way of chunking each task
* what you want as an output.

   For example, you could 'chunk' a textbook by chapters, and produce a set of index notes or construct a mindmap of key words as an output for each chapter. (See figure 2.4.)

c) Schedule tasks

Once you have manageable-sized tasks, plan when to do them. Use any method that works for you, e.g. journal, diary, calendar, mindmaps or spreadsheets. Whatever the method, paper-based or electronic, make sure you can use it to track your progress.

   Be realistic in your expectations. Make sure you understand the scope of each activity. Estimate how much time you have available, and remember to allow for breaks.

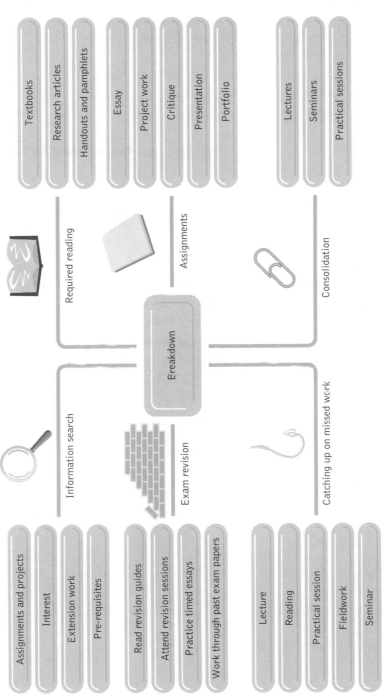

Figure 2.4 Breakdown of study tasks

- If you need to take time off for an important event near the time an assignment is due, try and spread your workload evenly over the couple of weeks leading up to the event.
- If an essay or project is due during an exam period, plan so you have time for both! Avoid an overload situation, where you end up writing your project at the expense of revision.

And of course, planning is only the first step. **You will need to follow through!**

TOP TIP

 When you've had a really successful study session, congratulate yourself . . . and then reflect on why it was so productive. Likewise, if you have a session and don't really feel you've achieved very much, think about why. Consider the environment you were in, your physical state, your mental state and whether you were following a study plan . . . and notice whether a pattern emerges.

SUMMARY

To help you get the most out of every study session, prepare properly. Pay attention to your:

- environment
- body
- mind
- study plan.

DANGER!

Have you ever noticed that sometimes, just as you're about to begin a study session, you feel a sudden urgency to spring-clean or sort through piles of stuff (clothes, bills, letters) which may have been lying around for ages? Your need to address this task before you study can be quite profound, and is frequently out of proportion to the task's actual importance. If this has a familiar ring to it, take comfort from the fact that it's a common way of delaying a task we don't particularly want to do (e.g. study). Pat's friend, Sue, dedicated three whole days to scrubbing all the woodwork in her flat with only two weeks to go before her final exams.

"Watch Out! . . . .
there's a displacement
activity about!"

These are called 'displacement activities', and some of us are experts in finding them just before we start to study. Recognising a desire for what it is can make it easier to resist side-tracking temptations.

And remember that even your study plan can become a displacement activity. Don't spend hours developing elaborate plans – allocate *only* the time needed to be productive.

3 Multiple Intelligences: Using All Your Strengths

KEY POINTS

- ☐ If you have self-doubt, you are almost certainly more capable than you think
- ☐ It is increasingly accepted that there are eight different kinds of intelligence
- ☐ We all have different combinations of strengths and weaknesses
- ☐ Understanding your natural strengths will help you make better use of them
- ☐ You can develop each of your intelligences, even those which are weak

INTRODUCTION

Have you ever wondered how smart you have to be to succeed? Imagine, just for a moment, what it would be like if you could learn to do anything and that the process of learning was both enjoyable and effortless. What would you learn? How would your life be different? Well, you almost certainly have more potential and natural ability than you previously thought. Many people have been amazed by the hidden talents of 'ordinary people' revealed in the television series 'Faking It'.

Historically, IQ has been regarded as very important, perhaps even the defining attribute in our education system. Educators widely accepted the notion that intelligence could be quantified by a single IQ

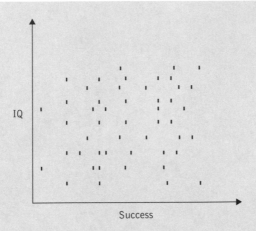

Figure 3.1 Relationship between IQ and success

measurement. The problem with this approach is that there is no evidence to suggest that IQ and success are correlated (see figure 3.1).

There are many examples of individuals who struggled with their formal education, yet went on to make outstanding contributions in their field. Thomas Edison didn't learn to read until he was nine years old, and was considered delinquent. Wernher Von Braun, the father of rocketry, failed 9th grade algebra. Einstein didn't speak until he was four, and had early difficulties with arithmetic (Moore 1981, pp. 2–3). Gandhi, one of the world's greatest leaders, acknowledged he was not a particularly good student, claiming 'I am an average man with less than average ability. I admit that I am not sharp intellectually.' (Quoted in Nanda 1985, p. 133.)

Howard Gardner's theory of multiple intelligences (1983) is changing the way we think about intelligence. It has expanded our horizon of available learning tools beyond the conventional linguistic and logical methods used by most students (e.g. textbooks, essays, formulas). There are now *eight* recognized intelligences (figure 3.2 overleaf) and it appears that each of them map to specific areas of the brain. Appreciating your own unique profile of strengths and weaknesses can help you apply different techniques and strategies to learn more effectively.

There are two ways you can apply the insights from this chapter:

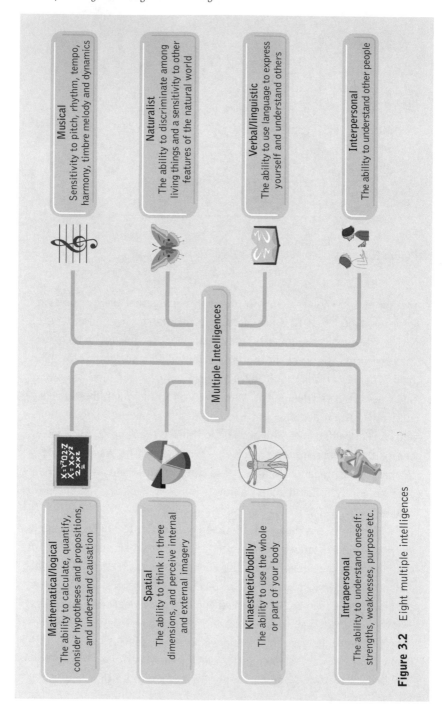

Figure 3.2   Eight multiple intelligences

1. Learn to use your current strengths in more circumstances and in more ways (see 'using your strengths' pages 56–8).
2. Work on your weaknesses, developing them into strengths (see figure 3.3 for a summary of ideas). Most of us have capacities in all of the intelligences, and can develop proficiency in each of them with appropriate encouragement, enrichment, and instruction.

IT WORKED FOR ME

'I used to type with two fingers, but it was very slow. So I learned to touch type. Now I use all my fingers I can type much faster and more accurately. It's the same with Multiple Intelligences. I used to use only two intelligences for my study, but now I use all eight. I find studying much easier, more fun, and my exam results have really improved.'

BEFORE YOU START

Make a list of 12–16 things you learned to do. These can be things you learned as an adult, but often you'll get a clearer insight by using examples from childhood. Here are some suggestions, but you should generate your own list: reading, riding a bike, singing songs, telling the time, cooking, typing, driving, playing guitar, canoeing, orienteering, salsa dancing, fossil collecting . . .

Now think about how the process of learning them felt to you, and make a note in figure 3.4. If you can't recall, perhaps ask an older family member if they remember.

Do you have anything in the fourth quadrant? These are your natural strengths. If they were in the school curriculum, you would probably get an 'A' for achievement and 'D' for effort. Our children (and their friends) regard these as the 'coolest' grades. However, sometimes when you can't remember how you learned to do something (because the process was so effortless) you might assume that everyone finds it easy. Many people often undervalue their

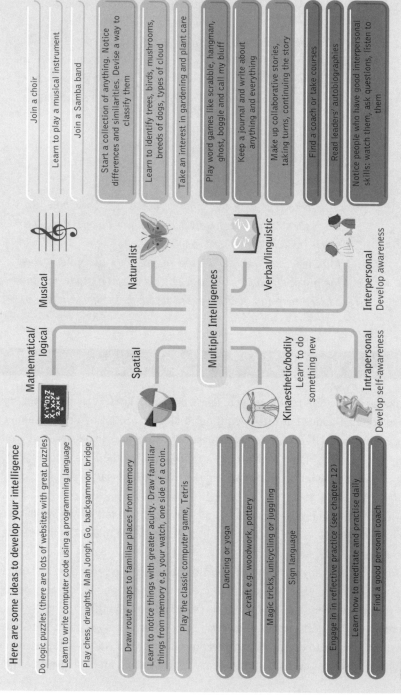

Here are some ideas to develop your intelligence

Mathematical/logical
- Do logic puzzles (there are lots of websites with great puzzles)
- Learn to write computer code using a programming language
- Play chess, draughts, Mah Jongh, Go, backgammon, bridge

Musical
- Join a choir
- Learn to play a musical instrument
- Join a Samba band

Naturalist
- Start a collection of anything. Notice differences and similarities. Devise a way to classify them
- Learn to identify trees, birds, mushrooms, breeds of dogs, types of cloud
- Take an interest in gardening and plant care

Spatial
- Draw route maps to familiar places from memory
- Learn to notice things with greater acuity. Draw familiar things from memory e.g. your watch, one side of a coin.
- Play the classic computer game, Tetris

Kinaesthetic/bodily
Learn to do something new
- Dancing or yoga
- A craft e.g. woodwork, pottery
- Magic tricks, unicycling or juggling
- Sign language

Verbal/linguistic
- Play word games like scrabble, hangman, ghost, boggle and call my bluff
- Keep a journal and write about anything and everything
- Make up collaborative stories, taking turns, continuing the story

Interpersonal
Develop awareness
- Find a coach or take courses
- Read leaders' autobiographies
- Notice people who have good interpersonal skills: watch them, ask questions, listen to them

Intrapersonal
Develop self-awareness
- Engage in in reflective practice (see chapter 12)
- Learn how to meditate and practise daily
- Find a good personal coach

Multiple Intelligences

Figure 3.3 Developing your multiple intelligences

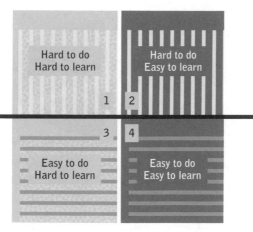

Figure 3.4 My learning process

strengths in category 4. Once you've explored the concept of MI, come back to your list, and see what, if anything, your category 4 items have in common.

Now let's take a look at each of the eight intelligences (figure 3.2). If you're interested in the criteria used to decide whether a dimension or attribute qualifies as an intelligence, see Appendix 1. There are eight widely accepted intelligences and some people believe there may be a ninth, Existential intelligence. In the following sections, we'll look at each of the eight intelligences in turn, and suggest some ways to use and develop them.

1. MATHEMATICAL/LOGICAL INTELLIGENCE

Core abilities: See figure 3.5 (overleaf) for mathematical/logical intelligence core abilities.

Mathematical/logical intelligence is highly valued in our education system, yet many adults considerably underestimate their talents in this area. If you profess to be 'hopeless' at maths, it's more likely you've not had the appropriate encouragement and help to develop your intelligence in this area.

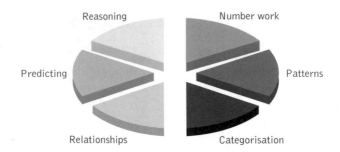

Figure 3.5   Mathematical/logical intelligence core abilities

We know much more now about how children learn maths, and how for many people early classroom experiences were in conflict with their natural learning style – sometimes with disastrous consequences.

You may use your mathematical/logical intelligence more than you realise. Do you do any of the following?

- Plan the sequence of jobs when redecorating a room e.g. painting the ceiling, walls, woodwork, replace the carpet etc.
- Plan journeys, using timetables.
- Budget your accounts/manage your finances.
- Estimate quantities.
- Gamble or play games of chance.
- Make risk assessments or predictions based on information.
- Make comparisons when you shop.

If you do any of the above, then you use your mathematical/logical intelligence. There are lots of ways you can use your mathematical intelligence in non-mathematical subjects. In many disciplines the ability to recognise patterns is extremely important, for example, with dates, plots, motives, themes, results, places, timings, and sentence structure. The ability to construct logical arguments (see chapter 10) and sequence steps or rank ideas is also extremely important.

'Although virtually all students enter school mathematically healthy and enjoying mathematics as they solve problems in ways that make sense to them, most exit school apprehensive and unsure about doing all but the most trivial mathematical tasks.'

Michael T. Battista (1999)

TRY THIS

Here's a thought. If you like formalising the structure or pattern in relationships, next time you come across a non-mathematical concept, why not try making up your own formula to explore some of the relationships between the elements. For example:

$$I = (2EI \times BL) + SF^2$$

Where:

I = Impact of writing BL = Beauty of language
EI = Emotional impact SF = Shock factor

Remember that it is not the accuracy of the formula itself that matters. What is important is that you find ways of processing information in the most helpful way *for you*.

2. VERBAL/LINGUISTIC INTELLIGENCE

Core abilities:

a)   Using words effectively either orally or in writing.

b)   The ability to manipulate:

- syntax or structure of language
- phonology or sounds of language
- semantics or meanings of language
- pragmatic dimensions or practical uses of language, including rhetoric, mnemonics, explanation, and meta-language.

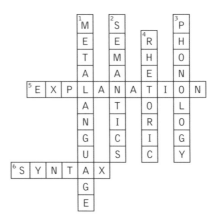

You use your verbal linguistic intelligence every time you read, write, tell or listen to a story. People with a highly developed verbal intelligence may enjoy playing with words, puns, mnemonics, and the sounds and structure of language.

DID YOU KNOW?

Our brains *love* metaphor. We are designed to learn about one thing in terms of another.

'*The essence of metaphor is understanding and experiencing one kind of thing in terms of another.'*
Lakoff & Johnson (1980)

TRY THIS

Choose a topic you are currently studying. Ask a friend to listen to you for 5–10 minutes while you complete the following sentence . . .

*The most important thing about **this topic** is. . . . **x***

Now answer the following question and go with the image that pops into your head, even if you have no idea how or why the two things are related.

*And **x** is like. . . .*

Your brain will have made non-verbal connections, which it can express in images.

If you trust it, and explore the images you will probably gain new insights about the topic. . . .

Go on and tell the story of how 'your picture' came to be. . . . what happened.

e.g. if **x** is like a book/flower, describe the pages/seed and how it came to be. Pay attention to the small details, the colour and texture of the cover/leaves, the setting, who wrote/watered it – as these can be very meaningful.

Q. *I'm a science student. How will linguistic intelligence be useful to me?*

A. Developing your linguistic intelligence will help you write up your notes as essays/book chapters/articles. From your notes, you can create your own crossword puzzles and use them to revise. Why not try some of the crossword construction packages which turn the solutions to your clues into a crossword? To help you remember factual information, why not make up your own creative stories containing key information, and embroider the story with rich detail. (See page 144, chapter 6.) You could share your stories with a 'study partner' as a revision strategy. And why not use metaphors to help you to understand in a richer, more complete way.

'One day my teacher insisted on changing the words I wrote because they "didn't make sense". To me they had been exactly right, but now I can't remember my original understanding.... I only remember that it is lost.'

Kimberly De Vries

3. BODILY/KINAESTHETIC INTELLIGENCE

Core abilities:

a)   Control of one's own body

b)   Control handling objects.

There are probably three distinct elements to this intelligence (Seitz 1989):

- the motor logic or neuromuscular skill that is involved in the syntax or ordering of movement
- kinaesthetic memory or the ability to mentally reconstruct muscular effort, movement, and position in space
- kinaesthetic awareness or awareness of posture, position, resistance, and the extent, direction and weight of movement.

Not all cultures value proficiency in all the intelligences equally. The !Kung bushmen of the Kalahari desert believe their intricate and complex medicine dance protects them from dark forces and so bodily kinaesthetic intelligence is highly valued. 'People learn the songs and dances when they are children and work for perfection in skill and timing all their lives.' (Thomas 1989, p. 125).

Q. How can I use this right now in my study?

- Writing and drawing are physical processes, so write up your notes and thoughts or capture them in drawings. If you use index cards, you can sort them physically. For more ideas, see chapter 8 on note-taking.
- Use your body as a metaphor, and use movement to capture information etc.
- Act out or dance the steps in a process.
- Use role play.
- Make up hand signs to represent facts or concepts.

4. SPATIAL INTELLIGENCE

Core abilities: Accurate mental visualisation and mental transformation of images.

We use our spatial intelligence to perceive and interpret shapes and images in 3D. When you think about the best route to get somewhere, you are using your spatial intelligence. The images in figure 3.6 (overleaf) are displaying the same data but in different ways. How easily can you mentally map the data from one image onto the others?

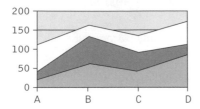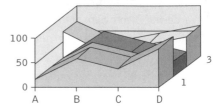

Figure 3.6   Spatial intelligence

Q. How can I use this right now in my study?

- Convert your notes into graphs and mindmaps. (There are a number of software packages available which make it very easy to create mindmaps. We like Mindjet's MindManager©).
- Explore relationships graphically, either in your mind or on paper.
- Imagine a way of physically navigating through a process or system, e.g. to learn about the circulation system, you could imagine navigating your way through the major veins, arteries and heart.
- Use the back of a jigsaw and write keywords or steps of a process on each piece, linking them in a meaningful way.
- Use a 'visual route' memory peg system (see chapter 7).

DANGER!

Spatial intelligence encompasses more than just visual images. There is widespread confusion between visual learning style and spatial intelligence. For example, many blind people display a high level of spatial ability. They can identify 2D and 3D shapes by touching them. Our blind friend, Cliff, has been known to provide the commentary on sightseeing coaches around his native city. Even without sight, he knows exactly where he is – demonstrating an impressive level of spatial intelligence.

'Multiple intelligences claims that we respond individually, in different ways to different kinds of content, such as language or music or other people. This is very different from the notion of learning style.* You can say that a child is a visual learner, but that's not a multiple intelligences way of talking about things. What I would say is, "Here is a child who very easily represents things spatially, and we can draw upon that strength if need be when we want to teach the child something new." '

Howard Gardner 1997 in Checkley, 1997

* See chapter 4

5. INTRAPERSONAL INTELLIGENCE

Core abilities: Awareness of own emotions, goals, feelings and motivation.

Intrapersonal intelligence is our cognitive ability to understand and sense our 'self': who we are, what feelings we have, why we are this way. It is not often recognised from the outside, unless perhaps it is expressed tangibly in some artistic form. Such people are likely to be realistic in what they can achieve and as such, are often valued colleagues and collaborators.

You can usually tell if you have a well-developed intrapersonal intelligence because you:

- are aware of your underlying anxieties, desires and motivations
- act on the basis of self-knowledge, creating environments, guiding behaviour, and making decisions based on an accurate picture of yourself

- possess a strong sense of identity and purpose, and make decisions based on what is right for you, not what is expected.

QUESTIONS FOR YOU

- What are your dreams? What is stopping you from achieving them? Does your 'list' include any of your personal attributes or limiting beliefs? If not, this might be a good place to start to develop your self-awareness.
- When was the last time you directed your anger to an 'innocent' person, who just happened to be in the wrong place at the wrong time? Self-awareness requires us to be honest with ourselves, about our underlying motivations and needs.

Q. How can I use this right now in my study?

You are already using this intelligence by reading this chapter. Learning about how you learn (sometimes called metalearning) is a great way to improve your effectiveness as a student.

Another tip is to ask yourself 'Why does this topic matter to me?' If the answer is not obvious, try and find a way of reframing a subject so that it becomes important to you. Learning is most effective when we have a connection with the subject.

6. INTERPERSONAL INTELLIGENCE

Core abilities: Awareness of emotions, goals, feelings and motivations of other people.

Many people with a well-developed interpersonal intelligence are good at resolving conflicts. They tend to be comfortable in the company of others, and are often natural leaders. The traits in Figure 3.7 are commonly associated with good interpersonal skills.

Are you sensitive to other people's facial expressions and voice?

Are you able to inspire others?

Are you able to discriminate between different interpersonal cues, and respond to them effectively?

Are you able to dispel other people's negative emotions and create positive energy?

Figure 3.7 Traits associated with well-developed interpersonal intelligence

IT WORKED FOR ME

'I used to think that studying meant sitting in my room by myself staring at piles of books. Then I found a study partner. We work really well together. We ask each other questions and test each other's knowledge. It is much more fun and the great thing is that I can remember the work we do together very easily.'

Q. How can I use this right now in my study?

- Teach what you have learned. Trying to explain something to someone really helps to clarify your own thinking . . . and getting stuck indicates where you haven't fully grasped something.
- Arrange team competitions and write your own questions.
- Organise co-coaching groups or pairs.
- Role play with groups of two, three or four.
- Find a 'study friend' and compare notes – you may be surprised by the different points you pick up and miss out. (This needs to be an active process.)

LOOKING AHEAD

Being 'people smart' is an increasingly valued asset in the workplace. Developing your interpersonal intelligence will help you with many skills including:

❉ *Influencing* ❉ *Coaching*
❉ *Negotiating* ❉ *Leading*
❉ *Communicating* ❉ *Managing*
❉ *Motivating* ❉ *Encouraging*
❉ *Collaborating*

7. MUSICAL INTELLIGENCE

Core abilities: see figure 3.8.

Infants as young as two months old are able to match pitch, melodic counter and loudness of their mother's voice. It seems that infants are predisposed to these aspects of music, even more than the core properties of speech – and musical intelligence may influence the emotional, spiritual and cultural development more than the other intelligences. (Gardner quoted in Black 1997.)

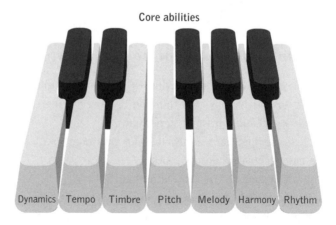

Figure 3.8   Musical intelligence core abilities

Q. *How can I use this right now in my study?*

- Make up your own songs and rhythmical poetry to summarise what you have learned.
- Associate different music with different topics.

At age 6, Pat remembers the day her music teacher gathered the class around the piano. She went round the children in turn, playing two notes and asking each child to sing the notes they had just heard. On the basis of this extensive assessment, Pat was told she couldn't join the school choir. This was common practice in the UK – and Pat, like thousands of other children, grew up with the firm belief that she 'couldn't sing'. As a teenager, she studied classical guitar and even won a music festival competition, but never had the courage to take any of the formal music exams because of her firm belief that she would fail the aural part.

We now know that letting any child believe they have no singing ability is misguided. The research suggests you can learn music at any age, though if you start later in life, it might take more time for you to reach proficiency (Jensen 2000).

And the good news is. . . .

There is significant evidence that developing your musical intelligence has benefits for some of the other intelligences, particularly the spatial and logical/mathematical intelligences.

8. NATURALIST INTELLIGENCE

Core abilities: see figure 3.9 (overleaf).

More recently, Gardner (1995) has added an eighth intelligence, the naturalist intelligence, to the original list of seven, though there is still some debate about how well this meets the requisite criteria outlined in appendix 1 (page 257). According to Gardner, individuals with highly developed naturalist intelligence are able 'to recognise flora and fauna, to make other consequential

Figure 3.9   Naturalist intelligence core abilities

distinctions in the natural world, and to use this ability productively.' Gardner speculates that this intelligence is used by suburban children when they sort and organise their collections of trading cards and the like.

Q. How can I use this right now in my study?

- Classify concepts/themes/facts/procedures/principles in as many ways as possible.
- Look for similarities and differences at lots of levels.
- Use matrix notes (see page 159).

DANGER!

There is a lot of misinformation about this intelligence. You may come across the notion that you engage your natural intelligence simply by going outside, having plants and fresh flowers in your work area, or displaying pictures of nature scenes. Well these things may impact on your emotional state, and as such they can play an important role in your learning effectiveness. But being outside does not, by itself, engage or develop your natural intelligence, any more than putting pictures of the number 7 around the room helps you engage or develop your mathematical logical intelligence. To develop your abilities in any area, you need to actively process information.

HOW DO I FIND OUT MY MULTIPLE INTELLIGENCE PROFILE?

The only Gardner-approved MI assessment at the time of writing is the Multiple Intelligence Developmental Assessment Scales (MIDAS) developed by Branton Shearer at Kent State University. According to Gardner, MIDAS was developed and validated in accordance with standard psychometric procedures, and includes careful guidelines about how to interpret and use the results.

However, unlike a standard IQ test, the MI results don't tell you how your intelligence level compares with the rest of the population – they are not norm-referenced. The results indicate where your strengths lie, but it would be misguided to try and rank yourself in comparison to other people.

Also, it's worth remembering that there are no standard attributes you must have to be considered intelligent in a specific area. There are several ways you can be intelligent within each category. So, for example, a highly linguistic person may be able to tell wonderful stories, but might not be able to read. Or a person with exceptional bodily/kinaesthetic intelligence may be a superb craftsman, but be unable to walk.

DANGER!

There are countless free inventories, quizzes and checklists on the web, which are of variable quality. Many are simply too short to be meaningful. As there are several ways you can be intelligent within each category, asking only two or three questions about each intelligence could easily produce misleading results. Many of the checklists confuse learning styles with multiple intelligences. Others seem to confuse 'liking' with 'proficiency'. Enjoying something is not the same as being good at it (Sternberg 1997). You may gain some useful insights into your individual MI profile by taking a few different quizzes, but be mindful of their potential limitations.

USING YOUR STRENGTHS

So, how can you use your natural strengths to help you? For most assignments and projects, there are many possible approaches, which draw on different intelligences. When tasked with an assignment or project, before you begin work, and even before you choose your option, think through all the possibilities in MI terms.

On pages 57 and 58 there are three examples for you to think about.

TAKE HEART

Why did the world celebrate the Jamaican bobsled team and Eddie 'the Eagle' Edwards in the 1988 Winter Olympics, and Eric 'the Eel' Moussambani in the 2000 Olympics? We suspect people were responding to the context of these athlete's achievements. In other words, intelligence is contextualised, which means that you need the right environment or context for intelligence to develop. You probably have potential in one or more of the intelligences that you have not had the opportunity to develop – either at all, or only partially. Once you recognise you have unmet potential, you can become more proactive in finding opportunities to develop that potential.

> 'Bobby Fischer might inherently have had the potential to be a great chess player, but if he had lived in a culture without chess, that potential would never have been manifested, let alone actualized.'
>
> Gardner 1991

Cultures value intelligences differently, often creating different opportunities for intelligences to flourish. For example, canoeing and swimming skills are highly valued by the Manus children of New Guinea. The seafaring Puluwat

Example 1: Economics

Suppose you are studying the law of supply and demand in economics. What would be the best way for you to utilise your natural strengths?

Approach	Intelligence
Explore the principles graphically	Spatial
Explore the mathematical formulae that express the relationship	Mathematical/logical
Reflect on what this means for each party involved	Interpersonal
Analyze your own probable reactions as a consumer and supplier	Intrapersonal
Find parallels in the natural world e.g. Predator/prey relationships	Naturalist
Read about the subject and/or give a presentation	Verbal/linguistic
Act out the principles of the law	Bodily/kinaesthetic
Write a song to express the principles of the law	Musical

Example 2: History

Suppose you are asked to write an essay/report/project about a particular historical battle.

Approach	Intelligence
Relevance of the landscape/geography/space	Spatial
Importance of sequencing of events or provision of other clues	Logical
Relationships between the key historical figures	Interpersonal
Analysis of how you, as one or more of the key players, might have felt and why you might have taken certain actions	Intrapersonal
Significance of season, weather, availability of food supplies	Naturalist
An analysis of the communication: clarity or confusion	Verbal & interpersonal
An account of your experience in a battle re-enactment	Kinaesthetic & intrapersonal

Example 3: English or Performing Arts

Suppose you are asked to write an essay/report/project about a film/play. The crossword clues below suggest some of the different approaches you might take to the assignment.

Across
5. An analysis of your emotional response to the work
6. A review of the staging/use of space
7. A review of the similarities and differences of the sub-plots/settings etc.
8. An analysis of the changing relationships between the characters

Down
1. A critique of the musical score
2. An analysis of the acting techniques and movement
3. The impact of the language and/or use of metaphor
4. An analysis of the sequence of events

(The answer is the multiple intelligence engaged by each approach. See page 259 for the answer.)

of the Caroline Islands are exceptional navigators, and place great emphasis on the development of spatial intelligence. Gambian mediators have
excellent interpersonal intelligence, which they use to successfully negotiate,
arbitrate or adjudicate disputes (Sheehan 1996).

MAKE IT EASY

According to Gardner, an essential insight is that not all intelligence is in
the head. In other words, intelligence is distributed. Productive individuals
rely heavily on the intelligence of other humans and non-human resources such
as books, computers and websites. How efficiently do you use the 'human'
resources available to you (colleagues, tutors, friends and family)? See chapter 5 for more information.

We suspect a huge amount of energy is wasted at all educational levels
trying to teach things in a way that doesn't make sense to the learner.

'*From an early age she loved pictures, especially in books
that were visually busy, like those by Richard Scarry . . . .
She grew to think of words as captions, as handles with
which to grab bulky trunks of reality. She never did learn
to sound out words, as she usually learned the whole word
all together, but she learned to fake it for school.*'

Kimberly De Vries

The author of the quote above talks about 'faking phonics'. This child learned
to read by recognising whole words, relating to their overall shapes rather
than breaking them down into composite parts. It appears that the teacher
required her to use phonics, even though they didn't make sense to her.
In MI terms, the child in the above quote probably had a highly developed
spatial intelligence. If this had been recognised, her natural abilities to think

spatially could have been harnessed in a variety of subjects, resulting in much more meaningful and easier learning. The pressure to conform may mean we are sometimes tempted to 'fake' the required response.

Why not discuss multiple intelligences with your tutor? A great deal has been written for teachers and educators about using multiple intelligences in the classroom. You may find some of your classes and projects are designed to address all intelligences. If so, look out for new ideas and approaches you can use.

LOOKING AHEAD

When you come to choosing your career, you may find it useful to consider whether your multiple intelligence profile matches the requirements of the job. Many adults are in jobs they don't particularly like. In many cases they've drifted into their careers because they were good at a particular subject at school. Take a look at the jobs listed in table 3.1. Which intelligences do you think they rely on? Go back to figure 3.4 and look at your natural strengths. If you can find a job that interests you *and* relies on your MI strengths, there is a better chance that you will achieve both success and fulfilment.

Table 3.1 Applying Multiple Intelligences to career choices

Job	Intelligences used
Accountant	
Actor	
Administrator	
Architect	
Fireman	
Journalist	
Lawyer	
Mechanic	
Sales manager	
Sculptor	
Taxonomist	
Translator	

SUMMARY

Competent students use their Multiple Intelligences wisely:

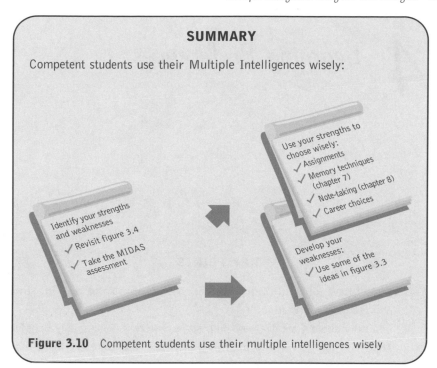

Identify your strengths
and weaknesses
✓ Revisit figure 3.4
✓ Take the MIDAS
assessment

Use your strengths to
choose wisely:
✓ Assignments
✓ Memory techniques
(chapter 7)
✓ Note-taking (chapter 8)
✓ Career choices

Develop your
weaknesses:
✓ Use some of the
ideas in figure 3.3

Figure 3.10   Competent students use their multiple intelligences wisely

4 Learning Preferences

KEY POINTS

- [ ] We all have different preferences in the way we like to take in, store and retrieve information
- [ ] Learning about your own learning style preferences has many benefits
- [ ] There are lots of ways to approach any task, and different tasks may benefit from different approaches
- [ ] No learning style preference is better than any other
- [ ] Looking ahead, you can apply your knowledge of learning styles at work

WHAT ARE LEARNING STYLES?

There is a lot of confusion in the literature about what exactly a learning style is and isn't. Learning styles are concerned with *how* you prefer to learn, and we don't all have the same approach. While we don't yet have '*the*' answer to 'How do people learn', we do know that 'learning' is 'learnable'.

Have you ever set up a gadget (new DVD player or video recorder perhaps) with someone who has a completely different approach? If your friend or partner needs to read the manual from cover to cover before doing anything, and you just want to press the buttons to see what happens, you might  find things get a bit tetchy. This may simply reflect the fact that you and your partner have different learning styles.

Although the evidence is not conclusive, it seems that some of our learning style preferences may be relatively stable over time and across situations, while others seem to be shaped by our experiences and the particular circumstances of the moment.

Sometimes we fall into the trap of believing our own approach is 'the best way', when what we really mean is that it's the best way *for us*! In reality, many different approaches can work. Ultimately, we hope this chapter will help you recognise that you have choices in the way that you approach any task.

If you want to know *why* it's important to understand your learning style preferences and the range of ways other people learn, here are eight good reasons:

1. Awareness of different learning styles can help you improve your grades or results, and the good news is that simply reading this chapter can help you! Reflecting on the ideas presented here, and trying to see how they apply in different situations will help you even more.

2. You can use your knowledge of your preferred learning styles to decide on the suitability of distance learning or an e-learning course. As with classroom-based courses, you're likely to do better when the material is presented in a style that matches your preference.

3. There is some evidence to suggest you may do better on courses where there is a match between your learning style and that of your teacher. You may not do so well if your learning styles are mismatched, and the material is not presented in ways that accommodate different learning styles. So, if you're not doing very well in a subject you love, and are tempted to drop the subject, bear in mind that you may be suffering from a mismatch of styles, not a lack of ability or potential!

4. You can apply learning-style theory to group-work: you can select roles which provide the best 'fit' for your strengths and preferences, and an understanding of individual differences can lead to greater tolerance, decreased conflict, improved teamwork and greater productivity.

5. Awareness of what 'works for you' and 'why it works' can help you make the best use of existing support (in tutorials, coaching or mentoring sessions) and help you clarify any need for additional support or information.

6. How you do in tests and assessments may depend on your learning-style preference and the type of assessment given, as well as your knowledge and ability.

7. You can improve the effectiveness of your communication. We tend to present information in the way we prefer to receive it. If you learn what this means for people who have learning styles that are different from yours, and accommodate them, your communication is likely to be more effective. So learning styles are relevant to all kinds of projects and assignments – both as a student and later in the workplace.

8. Some jobs and working environments are more suited to certain learning styles, so you can make your working life more productive by choosing work environments where there is a natural fit with your learning styles.

'I propose that the single most important and yet simple thing a teacher or parent can do for students is to give them the knowledge of what their learning style is and how to use it . . . When individuals understand more about themselves, they are able to produce at higher levels.'

Dr Lynn O'Brien

Because we all have a unique combination of talents, intelligences, learning styles and experiences, we bring slightly different perspectives to a situation or problem . . . so, as you read through this chapter, do keep in mind that each of these frameworks are only useful *to the extent that they help you*. And for each framework, we believe that the greater your natural bias towards one style, the more valuable it will be for you to learn about the other styles, and the greater the potential benefits from developing your less preferred styles.

LEARNING-STYLE FRAMEWORKS

Learning styles is a pretty big topic, and not surprisingly, lots of people have come up with their own models, which can get a bit confusing. Smith (1984)

DANGER!

Avoid the temptation to regard the result of any learning style assessment as definitive. Resist the temptation to latch on to any one model, and be aware of the limitations of each model/framework. Remember, there is no one framework or model that adequately covers all the different ways we learn. Regard this chapter as a starting point to thinking about how you learn, rather than an end point.

tabulated at least 17 learning-style inventories! Coffield et al. (2004a and 2004b) have just finished an 18-month project researching learning-style frameworks: they uncovered *over 50* different frameworks in current use, and investigated 13 of the most influential models in detail. The quality of research underpinning the models is variable, and there are still large gaps in what we know. We've chosen four of the better known frameworks to discuss here, and they are outlined in Figure 4.1.

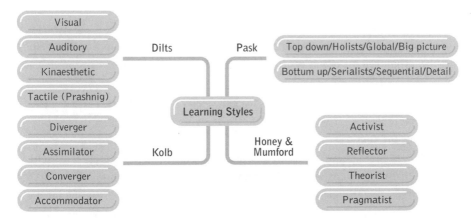

Figure 4.1 Learning-style frameworks

'TOP DOWN' OR 'BOTTOM UP'?

'Top Down' learners, sometimes referred to as Holist or Global learners, like to establish higher-ordered relationships and conceptualise the overall picture, rather than concentrate on the detail at any level. Holists may appear to have a 'scattergun' or 'globetrotting' approach to information and they like to make multi-discipline and multi-layered connections.

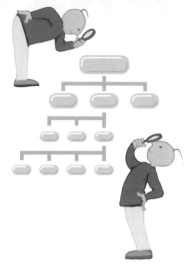

'Bottom up' learners are sometimes referred to as Serialist or Sequential learners. They like well-defined, ordered chunks of information presented in a linear sequence. They prefer to work through a framework step-by-step, concentrating on the details before conceptualizing the overall picture.

What's your preference?

What sort of approach have you taken with this book?

- Are you reading each page in sequence, each chapter in turn (a bottom-up approach), or have you dipped in and out, looking for snippets that help you build and expand your ideas in a range of related areas (a top-down approach)?
- Did you look at the mindmaps to understand the 'big picture' before you began reading, or would you prefer to study them more closely once you've read the text?
- Do you prefer to write essays that are full of detail (a bottom-up approach) or that explore connections, relationships and ideas (a top-down approach)?
- Do you prefer courses where the information is presented lesson by lesson in a well-structured hierarchy, with lots of detail (a bottom-up approach) or do you prefer 'big picture' overviews, with high-level information and anecdotes relating to other fields (a top-down approach)?

IT WORKED FOR ME

'Economics was my favourite subject at school, and I always found it very easy. I was quite shocked when I didn't do very well on my introductory course at Uni, and almost changed my major. I realise now that I'm a bottom-up, detail-person, and my tutor is definitely a top-down person, who finds all the detail quite irritating. Now I understand this, I structure my essays and assignments differently, and I always do a final edit to pare down the level of detail. My grades are much better, and my self-confidence has returned. I'm so relieved I didn't change my major!'

How can I use this information?

Because we tend to present information in the way that we like to learn ourselves, the majority of science, maths and computer courses are taught in a sequential, bottom-up – manner which can be difficult if you're a 'top down' or global learner. You could try asking lots of 'What if' questions as the answers may help you to build a broader picture of the subject matter, relating the detail to other wider concepts.

If you're a bottom-up learner being presented with information in a top-down way, you could try asking for a variety of very specific, detailed examples to illustrate the broader concepts.

'To deal with any situation successfully, you need to know *yourself* and how to handle your weaknesses; You also need to know *your style* and how to utilise your strengths.'

B. Prashnig

What's next

As we've already said, this is only *one* of a number of learning style frameworks and this distinction may not resonate with everyone: learners who flex effortlessly between top-down and bottom-up approaches may not find this particular distinction very helpful. So let's look at some of the other frameworks. . . .

HONEY & MUMFORD'S LEARNING STYLES

Honey and Mumford (1982) suggested there are four different learning styles, which they call activist, reflector, theorist, and pragmatist.

TRY THIS

To give you a very general idea of your preferences, answer the questions below. If you answer yes to three or four of the questions in any one section, you probably prefer that learning style (at least some of the time).

Theorist

Do you learn well:	Yes	No
• from situations where you need to think things through?	☐	☐
• from complex situations (e.g. business games) that last a long time?	☐	☐
• from models and theories?	☐	☐
• in interesting situations, even if they're not directly relevant?	☐	☐

Activist

Do you learn well: | Yes | No

- from new experiences and hands-on activities? ☐ ☐
- through role play and business games? ☐ ☐
- in situations which are exciting and full of drama? ☐ ☐
- when you're 'thrown in at the deep end'? ☐ ☐

Pragmatist

Do you learn well: | Yes | No

- from exercises with an explicit or obvious link to your work? ☐ ☐
- from practical, relevant activities? ☐ ☐
- in situations when implementing the learning is important? ☐ ☐
- by drawing up 'action plans'? ☐ ☐

Reflector

Do you learn well: | Yes | No

- from activities where you can observe other people first? ☐ ☐
- when you've sufficient time to think things through? ☐ ☐
- from activities where you're not told exactly what to do? ☐ ☐
- by discussing ideas with other people? ☐ ☐

DANGER!

In any team or project, the Theorists and Reflectors (or assimilators) are likely to take more time at every stage than the Activists or Pragmatists are happy with. Unless this is acknowledged and managed in a supportive way, it can lead to increasing conflict as the project progresses.

Practical application: Information-searching skills

There is no published research supporting this model. However, it has been used extensively over the years, and anecdotally, a lot of learners have found it useful. Sheila O'Flynn (2003) worked with hundreds of scientists at Unilever, helping them to improve their information-searching skills. She observed a strong correlation between the way they approached (and conducted) their information searches and their preferred learning styles. And once the scientists become aware of their own learning styles, their searching skills improved.

For most students, finding information efficiently is crucially important, e.g. when making literature reviews, searching for material for term papers, or simply for background reading. Broadly speaking, there are four stages to any information search:

1. Question formulation or clarification of the information need.
2. The search itself.
3. The analysis of the search results.
4. The communication of findings.

So, let's take a closer look at how you can apply Honey & Mumford's learning styles to your information-searching skills.

Do you recognise yourself in any of these descriptions?

The theorist

- Conducts very thorough literature searches, and likes to re-read findings . . . just to be sure
- Enjoys deconstructing the question and analyses related aspects and concepts
- Likes the detail about exactly how the syntax works in each database, and often uses sophisticated syntax for searching, e.g. uses truncations and wildcards
- Enjoys searching primary sources
- May be regarded by others as information experts, but once recognised as such, may not be able to see their own gaps
- Analyses and assimilates lots of information and produces useful generalisations
- May be reluctant to write up findings, especially if the analysis is not completely finished
- Is sometimes inclined to communicate data rather than insights.

TOP TIPS FOR THEORISTS

- Recognise your tendency to delay coming to a conclusion, and 'keep on searching'. Avoid endlessly collecting references.
- Learn to set clear deadlines for yourself about when to stop searching – and stick to them!
- Practise submitting your results within tight deadlines, even if the analysis isn't as complete as you would like.

The activist

- Prefers informal approaches to information-gathering e.g. talks to the person down the hall, or by the coffee machine. Adopts a 'Phone a friend' approach in preference to a structured search methodology
- Tends to have excellent networks. Is sometimes referred to as the 'information gateway'
- Is likely to discuss the 'problem' with colleagues as a way of understanding it
- Is likely to dip into the most easily available relevant source (Google's 'Feeling Lucky' button was developed for activists)
- Tends to avoid detail, and rarely reads documentation e.g. 'Help' or 'FAQ'
- Is reluctant to search multiple sources
- Prefers simple models that capture key ideas in an accessible form
- Is often impatient with conflicting data
- Is excellent at communicating progress and findings through their networks
- Often postpones writing up a report, and when they finally get round to it, they often have a minimalist approach to detail and documentation e.g. references and data.

TOP TIPS FOR ACTIVISTS

- Learn how to clarify your information need when there is no-one to talk to (for example, playing with synonyms, and spend more time identifying key words for the search).
- Don't read a broad overview and accept it as definite.
- Avoid one-stop shopping: Make sure you search multiple sources.
- Learn how to search key databases effectively: do the online training session, read the 'Help' and 'FAQ', or ask a librarian or information expert to show you.
- When communicating the results of your search, pay attention to the context and provide detail in the way of references and data.

DANGER!

Activists can talk very convincingly about how thorough their search was . . . which is true *by their standards*. They are often unaware of the limitations of their searching methods. This is a potential danger for 'activist journalists', for example.

The pragmatist

- Tends to be very focused on 'getting something done', is very keen to get started and will probably pick the keywords very quickly, with minimal thought
- Is likely to eliminate extraneous concepts or aspects to keep the question manageable
- Will focus on solving a problem rather than developing or complicating it
- Likes to have a master set of search terms to be used across all sources rather than develop a search for each source separately
- Adopts a very pragmatic approach e.g. uses databases which are readily available rather than those which may be most suitable
- Tends to focus on secondary sources (summaries and encapsulations of knowledge), and is often reluctant to delve into primary literature to confirm or question 'perceived wisdom'
- Isn't usually concerned with the detail underlying search syntax
- Is likely to finish the write-up, but the reports tend to be very short and to the point. Often reports are not contextualised and may not have a very full list of references.

TOP TIPS FOR PRAGMATISTS

- Recognise your tendency to 'speed' through each stage of the search process, and consider whether more time might enhance the quality of results.
- Spend more time defining your information need, and exploring alternative search words.
- Consider developing and complicating a problem before you move into 'solution' mode.
- Learn to recognise when primary sources are appropriate and learn to use them.
- Avoid drawing conclusions based on insufficient information.
- When you are presenting the results of your search, think about what might be relevant in the future – not just what's relevant now.

The reflector

- Is likely to analyse the question thoroughly and is usually able to 'distil the essence' of the problem into a well-formulated question
- Doesn't rush to start a search. Usually takes time to assimilate what is known first
- Easily resists the temptation to use a source just because it's convenient. Usually tries to understand the resources being used
- Uses secondary sources effectively to establish what is known, and then uses primary sources to complete the picture
- Is usually very good at structuring the results of the search
- Will not rush the analysis
- Is usually happy to write up a detailed analysis and report, but may resist producing simple or generalised versions.

TOP TIPS FOR REFLECTORS

- You may have difficulty meeting deadlines, because of your preference for thoroughness. Consider whether reducing the time spent will really impact on the quality of the results.
- Recognise when it is sufficient to review secondary sources and avoid the temptation to delve into primary sources unless the 'problem' specifically warrants it.
- Practise producing simplified or generalised summaries e.g. 'executive reports' – even if they seem over-simplified to you!

VAKT (VISUAL, AUDITORY, KINAESTHETIC, TACTILE) LEARNING-STYLE FRAMEWORK

Robert Dilts developed another approach to learning styles, which evolved from the observation that we have different sensory preferences for receiving, processing and using information. Dilt's original model (and the one most often referred to), suggests people differ in their preferences for visual (V), auditory (A) and/or kinaethestic (K) information. More recently, Prashnig has argued for a distinction between kinaesthetic (K) and tactile (T) learners, because, although frequently the preferences for 'whole-body learning' and 'touch learning' are linked, they can be completely independent.

To give you an idea of your sensory preferences, answer the following questions and add up the number of V, A, K and T 'preferences.'

	Yes	VAKT preference
1. I can clearly picture things in my head.		V
2. My notes have lots of pictures, graphs etc. in them.		V
3. In a test, I can 'see' the textbook page and the correct answer on it.		V
4. When reading, I listen to the words in my head or read aloud.		A
5. I'd rather listen to a tape than have to read it in a book.		A
6. I talk to myself when I'm problem-solving or writing.		A
7. I can concentrate better when music is playing		K
8. My desk and cupboards look disorganized.		K
9. I like to move around when I'm studying; it helps me think.		K
10. Doodling helps me to concentrate.		T/V
11. I like to play with pens and other objects when I'm thinking.		T
12. When choosing clothes, the 'feel' of the fabric is most important.		T

We know that babies rely very heavily on touch to explore their world, and a significant proportion of primary school children have a 'kinaesthetic' preference. In most primary schools, the teaching methods accommodate kinaesthetic and touch-dependent learners. By contrast, many secondary schools rely almost exclusively on visual and auditory methods, and tertiary institutions rely predominantly on auditory teaching methods. The situation is changing, but it is still true that in general, kinaesthetic and tactile learners are disadvantaged in traditional higher education.

You may come across the widely quoted figures that 65 per cent of the population are visual learners, 30 per cent are auditory and 5 per cent are kinaesthetic. However, the situation is more complex than these figures suggest. For example, published figures indicate that the proportion of adults and secondary school children with K/T preferences in New Zealand is much higher than in the US (Prashnig 1998). It is interesting to reflect on whether our 'don't touch' cultures might result in adults repressing their tactile learning-style preference for more acceptable visual and auditory ones, and, if this is happening, what effect might this have on overall learning effectiveness.

Visual learners

Visual learners relate most effectively to written information, notes, diagrams and pictures. Typically they will be unhappy with a presentation where they are unable to take detailed notes – to an extent information does not exist for a visual learner unless it has been seen written down. This is why some visual learners will take notes even when they have printed course notes on the desk in front of them. Visual learners will tend to be most effective in written communication, symbol manipulation, and so on.

Q. How can I use this right now in my study?

- In lectures and presentations, try sitting furthest from the door and window and toward the front of the class, if possible. Look at the person while he or she is talking, to help you to stay focused. Ask a teacher to explain something again when you don't understand a point being made. Ask to borrow the tutor's notes to fill in any gaps in your own notes.
- When you're taking notes and revising, write things down, **even** if you are given handouts, because you remember them better that way (quotes, lists, dates, etc.). Use colour to highlight the main ideas in your notes, textbooks, handouts, etc. Experiment with mindmaps, picture notes and symbols (see chapter 8). Many visual learners study better by themselves, in a quiet place. However, you might want to experiment with music, especially if you're studying maths, or mathematically related topics.

Auditory learners

Auditory learners relate most effectively to the spoken word. They will tend to listen to a lecture, and then take notes afterwards, or rely on printed notes. Often information written down will have little meaning until it has been heard – it may help auditory learners to read written information out loud. Auditory learners may be sophisticated speakers, and may specialise effectively in subjects like law or politics.

Q. *How can I use this right now in my study?*

Try studying with a friend so you can talk to each other and hear the information. Recite things you want to remember out loud (quotes, lists, dates, etc.). Ask your lecturers if you can give an oral report instead of written work. Make tape cassettes of classroom lectures, or read class notes onto a tape, and then listen to the tape to revise. Read aloud whenever possible.

Kinaesthetic learners

Kinaesthetic learners learn effectively through whole-body movement, and learn skills by imitation and practice. Adult kinaesthetic learners are frequently forced to deal with information that is *not* presented in a manner that suits them.

Q. *How can I use this right now in my study?*

You learn best by doing, moving, or hands-on experiences, and may find it difficult to concentrate when sitting still. In some formal lectures, it may be possible to stand at the back, and perhaps pace a few steps. It may be helpful to explain to your tutor that this will help you to concentrate. If it is not possible to stand or move around, you could try crossing your legs and bounce or jiggle the foot that is off the floor.

When memorising information, try writing the information in the air or on a desk or carpet with your finger. Picture the words in your head as you do this. Later, when trying to recall this information, close your eyes and recall how you wrote the word in the air. Try pacing or walking around while reciting to yourself or looking at a list or index card. Or mentally review concepts while cycling/running. Find a 'study partner' who also likes being active when reviewing material. e.g. throw/kick a ball to each other, the thrower asks a question for the recipient to answer. If you have a stationary bicycle, try reading while pedalling. Some bicycle shops sell reading racks that will attach to the handlebars and hold your book.

Tactile learners

 Touch-dominant learners find that tactile sensations help them to concentrate. They find it difficult to keep their hands still and have a strong desire to explore shapes and textures, for example by touching sculptures. The way something feels is more important that how it looks.

Q. *How can I use this right now in my study?*

- If you are asked to watch a demonstration, or slide show, volunteer to 'help' with the set-up. Perhaps you could explain to your tutor that you are a 'touch-dependent' learner, and ask them to help identify appropriate hands-on opportunities for you.
- If you use index cards for notes and revision, perhaps try ways of making them 'feel' different, for example using pinking shears, or embossing tools. You can also try and link information mentally to the feel of different materials.
- If you are in a formal classroom setting, try keeping a stress ball, or 'bean bag' toy in your pocket to 'play with' unobtrusively.

> 'We might lose any of one or more of the other senses – sight, hearing, smell, for instance – but to lose an ability to feel, that is, touch, is to lose all sense of being in a world, and fundamentally of being at all.'
>
> Paul Rodaway

DANGER!

Be aware that for some people this type of 'tactile play' is distracting and reduces their concentration. If you're not sure about your preference, try it and see . . . but be honest with yourself if you find tactile toys simply provide relief when you're bored!

KOLB'S LEARNING STYLES

Kolb's (1984) theory of experiential learning is widely used today, and is based on the premise that learning is a cyclical process, with four phases, colloquially known as watching, thinking, doing and feeling. These phases are based on two dimensions: a) active versus reflective information-processing, and b) concrete or abstract perceptions. These two dimensions are divided into quadrants, which form Kolb's learning styles (accomodator, diverger, assimilator and converger), as shown in figure 4.2.

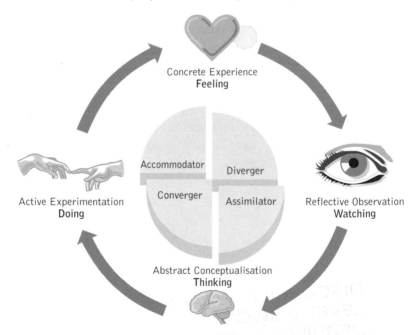

Figure 4.2 Kolb's learning styles

The take-home message is that if you become proficient at learning throughout the cycle, and can flex between all four learning styles, you will be a much more effective 'learner' – which is obviously a good thing! Like all models, this is probably over-simplified, and it is debatable whether all learning goes through the full cycle – and indeed, all learning may not be cyclical – but the framework is widely used because many people find it helpful.

See if you recognise yourself based on these descriptions of the learning styles.

* **Divergers** tend to conceptualize things in concrete terms and process information reflectively. They enjoy situations that call for generating a wide range of ideas e.g. brainstorming sessions, tend to have broad cultural interests and like to gather information, are able to view concrete situations from a variety of viewpoints and generally observe situations first before taking action.

  In terms of instructional situations, these learners prefer situations that allow them to observe, such as lectures or reading, and that provide concrete examples.

* **Assimilators** rely on abstract concepts and use reflective processing. They are able to take a wide range of information and put it into concise, logical form, are often less focused on people and more interested in abstract ideas and concepts and generally find it more important that a theory has logical soundness than practical value.

  In an instructional situation, they prefer instruction that is organised and structured; they enjoy reading and developing theories, and probably enjoy keeping a learning log or journal.

* **Accommodators** rely on the concrete concepts, but are active processors. In solving problems, they tend to act on 'gut' feelings rather than on logical analysis, and usually rely more heavily on people for information than on their own technical skills.

  In instructional situations, these learners enjoy fieldwork and prefer learning from 'hands-on' experiences.

* **Convergers** also use abstractions, but are active processors of the information. These individuals are able to find practical uses for ideas and theories. They tend to be problem-solvers and make decisions based on finding solutions to questions or problems, and would rather deal with

technical tasks and problems than with the social and interpersonal issues.

They prefer instructional settings that have practical application and allow them to solve problems.

TOP TIP

Students who can flex between all of the learning styles will have a definite advantage. Anecdotally, we know it is hard to change your learning style preferences, but **awareness** and **practice** are the key ingredients!

Think about how you typically go about learning something, for example, how to use a new piece of software. Make a note of your learning style preference(s) for this task, and decide to try a different approach next time (see figure 4.3).

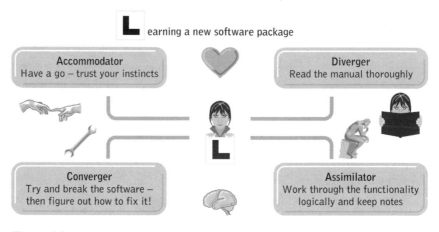

L earning a new software package

Accommodator
Have a go – trust your instincts

Diverger
Read the manual thoroughly

Converger
Try and break the software –
then figure out how to fix it!

Assimilator
Work through the functionality
logically and keep notes

Figure 4.3   Learning a new software package

LOOKING AHEAD

Cook (in press) discusses that although the research suggests that the natural science curriculum (medicine, biology, physical science and mathematics) favours convergers and assimilators, half the students in these majors are pursuing disciplines where their learning style is not preferred . . . and goes on to suggests that:

'perhaps the large proportion of students who drop out of biology and premed/dental programs are mismatched with the desired learning styles of the professions they are entering.'

Loo (2002) used the Kolb framework to look at learning styles of several hundred hard and soft business majors. He found that the 4 styles were equally represented among the 'soft' majors, but among the hard majors, there was a significantly higher proportion of 'assimilators', and lower proportion of accomodators and divergers.

So, this suggests that there may be a 'fit' between certain learning styles and some disciplines and professions . . . and you might want to use this to inform your career choices!

Q. How are learning styles different from intelligences?

A. People often confuse learning styles and intelligences. A useful indication of whether something is a style or an intelligence, is to ask yourself whether 'more is always better'. If it is, then it is probably an intelligence. If it depends, then it is probably a learning style, because each learning style has advantages in certain situations, and there isn't one style which is 'better' overall or 'more desirable' than the others.

TRY THIS

Can you see any overlap between the different frameworks we've presented here?
Which ones make the most intuitive sense to you?
Jot down your ideas here:

SUMMARY

- People prefer to receive and process information in many different ways
- Unlike intelligences, learning styles are about 'fit'. Each style has advantages in different settings
- Finding out about your own learning-style preferences can help to use your natural strengths to improve your performance
- Understanding learning styles can help you to respect individual differences and capitalise on the strengths of each learning style
- You can apply your knowledge of learning styles in the workplace.

5 Working with others

KEY POINTS

- [ ] Working successfully with others is an increasingly important student skill
- [ ] Group-work presents different challenges from those of individual study
- [ ] At least four areas contribute to successful group-work: goal focus, roles, processes and interactions
- [ ] On-line group activities raise some different issues than face-to-face activities
- [ ] Others can help you to become a successful learner

INTRODUCTION

In this chapter, we consider some benefits and challenges of working as a team before exploring five areas that contribute to project success. These are shown in figure 5.1 (overleaf).

After this we look at some of the unique challenges that online groups face, and we'll finish by exploring some of the ways others can help you to learn successfully.

In recent years the purpose of further and higher education has been increasingly under the spotlight. One outcome of this scrutiny has been the introduction of terms such as 'key skills', and 'employability skills'.

The UK Qualifications and Curriculum Authority (QCA) has identified 'working with others' as a key 'employability skill' and if we

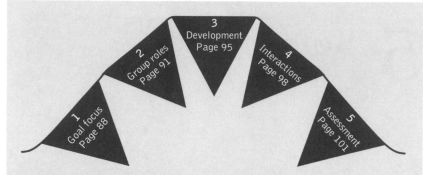

Figure 5.1 Five factors that contribute to project success

combine this concept with the continued drive for student-centred learning, rather than teacher-centred, then we reach:

Transferable people skills + Student-centred learning = Group-work

One differentiation between groups and teams is that teams are supposed to have shared goals, whereas members of a group may have different and sometimes conflicting goals.

Successful project work requires working as a team and is our focus in this chapter. By *group project* we mean an assignment typically undertaken by 6–10 students and usually extending over a period of several weeks.

As a student you may encounter several other forms of group activity, which vary in size, formality and duration, including:

- tutorials
- seminars
- classroom-based practical exercises, e.g. laboratory experiments, music groups
- classroom-based small-group work, e.g. brainstorming exercises
- support groups.

Many of the issues we raise in the following sections apply to each of these, even though in tutorials or seminars, for example, individuals may have different goals.

How do you feel about group-work?

How do you feel about working with others on joint projects? Does it generate feelings of excitement and enthusiasm or does it make you feel uneasy and wish for an opportunity to work alone? In our experience, many students are quite negative about group projects. Working alone means you have sole responsibility for your learning and sometimes it may seem less efficient to work with others. However, when group-work goes well, there are additional rewards (Bourner et al. 2001, Mills 2003).

TRY THIS

Take some time now to identify the possible benefits and drawbacks of undertaking a group project (see Table 5.1, overleaf).

Our list in Table 5.1 (overleaf) is pretty evenly balanced. What does your list look like? With such a fine balance, what can you do to promote the benefits and lessen the disadvantages? Let's take a closer look at the five aspects of group work that we referred to earlier.

1. GOAL FOCUS

The transformation from loose groups of individuals to effective teams takes both time and skill (Sheard and Kakabadse 2002). In project work, everyone must work together as an effective team. Drawing up a project plan or management checklist near the start of the project helps to ensure that the team:

- clarifies the team goal
- clarifies the amount of time and effort required
- clarifies and allocates specific responsibilities and tasks.

INTERESTING FINDING

McGuire and Edmondson (2001) analysed the evaluations of more than 50 students who had participated in small group projects. 36 stated they would choose to work in a group for their next project, if the choice was available. The main reason for opting out of group-work was the desire to take individual responsibility for the grade achieved. Only one student did not want to be involved in more group-work in the future.

Table 5.1   Benefits and drawbacks of group assignments

Benefits of group assignments	Drawbacks of group assignments
• Others can contribute different knowledge and perspectives	• There is a loss of personal control
• You can allocate tasks according to the skills within the group	• Reliance on others who you may not know or like
• Working with others can increase motivation	• Group members may have different standards, expectations and abilities
• You learn through the discussion and debate	• There is a danger of under-achieving unless everyone pulls their weight
• Working with others can be a positive and fun experience	• Grading the project is more difficult
• You can be more adventurous in how you choose to tackle the assignment than you might be by yourself	• Project management is more difficult
	• Not knowing everyone may preclude skill optimisation
• Working in groups is a 'real-life' skill!	• Consensus decisions may be difficult and time-consuming to reach
• Group assignments provide an apportunity for socialising and for friendships to develop	• Project management can become slow and unwieldy
	• Groups tend to make more 'risky' decisions than individuals
	• There may be personality clashes
	• Working with others can decrease motivation

A well-designed project plan helps to keep everyone focused on the goal and it provides a benchmark against which you can monitor progress.

A project plan typically involves a number of stages (see figure 5.2). A project management checklist is a rational plan of action. Try to treat it as a living document – refer to it often and be prepared to modify it as the project develops.

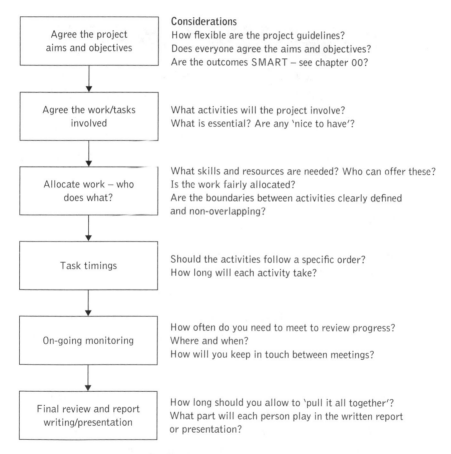

Considerations

Agree the project aims and objectives
How flexible are the project guidelines?
Does everyone agree the aims and objectives?
Are the outcomes SMART – see chapter 00?

Agree the work/tasks involved
What activities will the project involve?
What is essential? Are any 'nice to have'?

Allocate work – who does what?
What skills and resources are needed? Who can offer these?
Is the work fairly allocated?
Are the boundaries between activities clearly defined and non-overlapping?

Task timings
Should the activities follow a specific order?
How long will each activity take?

On-going monitoring
How often do you need to meet to review progress?
Where and when?
How will you keep in touch between meetings?

Final review and report writing/presentation
How long should you allow to 'pull it all together'?
What part will each person play in the written report or presentation?

Figure 5.2 Project management checklist

TOP TIP

Successful group work requires a balance between 'good people skills' and 'good project management' skills. When the two are brought together effectively, the experience is likely to be enjoyable and productive. Are you and your group considering both?

2. GROUP ROLES

Most people, if asked to form groups, will gravitate towards their friends. Is that what you do? By doing this you remain within your 'comfort zone' – you know and like the people you work with and you are aware of their skills. Yet working with friends also brings some potential disadvantages, including:

- You may not have the best mix of people for the job – particularly if we choose friends who are similar to ourselves
- As a group you may become too relaxed, easy going or uncritical
- You may waste time through chitchat and socialising rather than getting on with the task
- There are fewer opportunities to develop your own people skills if you always work with the same people
- Choosing your own team does not mimic many 'real-life' situations.

Student project teams tend to be either friendship groups, randomly allocated teams (e.g. by allocating numbers in the classroom) or teacher allocated.

Belbin (2003) observed groups of managers attempting to solve specific business problems and suggested that the most effective teams contain people who, between them, are able to occupy nine different roles. Although there may be a danger of over-emphasising the importance of roles, our suggestion is to try and work with members' role preferences whenever you can. People tend to be more motivated when they are occupying a role they enjoy, and it can be helpful to explore this during the planning stage when the responsibilities are being assigned.

Each Belbin role has been associated with some distinct skills that contribute positively to the group functioning and also some potential weaknesses

Table 5.2 Belbin's nine roles

The nine identified roles and associated skills	The nine identified roles and potential weaknesses
Plant: An imaginative problem-solver, the creative thinker who looks at topics in a new way	**Plant:** May disregard detail and not consider the practical implications of new ideas
Co-ordinator: Clarifies issues, keeps everyone on target, confident and delegates the workload	**Co-ordinator:** May be seen as lazy, avoiding work or manipulating others, which may result in group tension
Monitor-evaluator: Considers all options, is pragmatic and shows good judgment, evaluative and analytical	**Monitor-evaluator:** May not be able to motivate others: appears dull and unexciting
Implementer: Practical – makes things happen. Organised and efficient	**Implementer:** Inflexible and may be resistant to new approaches or new ideas
Completer-finisher: Attends to detail, is conscientious and delivers on time	**Completer-finisher:** May be anxious, 'nagging', nit-picking and unwilling to delegate
Resource investigator: Enthusiastic, follows up new ideas and is good at networking	**Resource investigator:** Liable to become bored and so lose interest quickly
Teamworker: Perceptive, averts friction, listens, and manages the emotional state of the team	**Teamworker:** Finds it difficult to make decisions, especially when under pressure
Specialist: Single minded, provides scarce knowledge and is a self-starter	**Specialist:** Contributes narrowly and may not be that interested in team success
Shaper: Challenges ideas, works well under pressure, overcomes obstacles, and is good at prioritising	**Shaper:** Can be overbearing, bossy and impatient! May upset others

(see table 5.2). In a well-performing team, individual members can moderate their behaviours to prevent these weaknesses occurring. The table summarises the best and worst of each role so it is really quite an 'extreme' summary. Even so, can you see yourself in any of these simplified descriptions?

Groups with a concentration of mainly one role may experience problems working together. How do you imagine a group of mainly plants would behave, for example? It is likely to generate novel and imaginative ideas but the group may struggle to evaluate them or implement actions!

INTERESTING FINDING

A study comparing the effectiveness of 'mixed' versus 'shaper' groups found that although the shapers had more group interaction, they were less likely to identity either the key objectives or the details that needed to be addressed, or reach a consensus (Prichard & Stanton 1999).

These nine roles can be grouped together in different ways. Figure 5.3 shows one way of doing this:

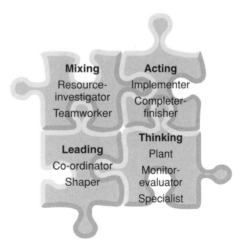

Figure 5.3   Role groupings

They can also be grouped in other ways. For example, using Kolb's Learning Style Preferences (see page 80), you could group the roles into: Thinking (plant, specialist, monitor-evaluator), Feeling (teamworker, and resource-investigator), Watching (co-ordinator) and Doing (implementer and completer-finisher). The important point is to consider role mix and balance when forming a group.

If you are interested in finding out your own preferred role(s) you could ask whether your college or workplace has purchased rights to administer the Belbin questionnaire – many have! There is also an official Belbin web-site that you might want to look at.

DANGER!

A natural preference for a given role(s) is no guarantee that the role will be performed well. Mental ability, values and social skills also matter. The ideas generated by a plant, for example, may not all be good ideas!

THINGS TO THINK ABOUT

- You can be comfortable in more than one of the Belbin-defined group roles – or you may have a strong tendency to occupy just one of the roles.
- You can improve your performance in roles that do not fit your strongest tendencies through experience and effort.
- You may feel unfulfilled if you are continually allocated to roles that are not a natural fit.
- A group is more than the sum of the parts. Some roles may sound sexier than others, but without role balance then things are more likely to go wrong.

Leadership

Leadership involves influencing the behaviours of others in order to reach a mutual goal and is important to the success of any project. Two of the Belbin roles are defined as 'leadership roles', and they complement each other: The shaper leads through 'direction and vision' while the co-ordinator leads through 'guiding and delegation'. Other approaches to leadership have been identified outside Belbin's work (Adair 1989, Kouzes and Posner 2003).

How do you think the role of leader is best achieved? Do you think there is a difference between leading and managing? Do you identify anyone as a leader in your project groups? If so, what is their leadership style? What type of leader would you be? Thinking about these issues now is useful not only for your project work but also in the workplace. Did you know that many organisations identify leadership training as their highest training priority?

3. GROUP DEVELOPMENT

Tuckman (1965) reviewed the empirical evidence and proposed that groups typically pass through four different developmental stages. These are:

Stage 1 Forming

At this stage group members have just come together and are typically feeling uncertain and anxious. They are probably seeking direction and clarity about what is expected and conversation tends to be polite and neutral. Typically, not much is achieved at this stage towards the project objectives.

Stage 2 Storming

During this stage members are clarifying roles and protocol within the group. This may involve challenge, debate and discussion. Sub-groups may form and there may be attempts to develop a 'hierarchy' within the group or to challenge the leader or leadership style. Typically this period involves a period of tension or discomfort.

Stage 3 Norming

At this point all group members start to model the 'agreed' behaviours, which paves the way for productive work. Accepted ways of working are established, work gets under way and members begin to feel that they share a common bond.

Stage 4 Performing

The group now focuses on the task in hand. Energy is directed at the goal and not at internal disputes. Accepted but non-rigid patterns of working develop and this is the most productive and industrious stage.

Sometimes people include a fifth stage, at the end of the task or when the goal has been completed. It is called 'Adjourning' and is characterised by emotion stemming from the sense of 'moving on'.

TRY THIS

Think about some of the groups that you are involved with through your study.

1. Do you recognise any of the processes described here?
2. What stage do you think each group is currently in?

Although other models of group development exist, the Tuckman model has been widely utilised across a range of settings and types of research (Gersick 1988, Whelan 2003, Mackenzie 1997). It considers developmental stages (rather than group functions) but has been criticised for not considering the dimension of time. How well does this model match your own experiences with groups?

How can I use this model?

Being alert to possible developmental stages may help your group pass through them smoothly. For example:

- During the forming stage you can facilitate introductions, ice-breakers, opportunities for social exchanges, goal clarification and ground rules (see page 98).
- During the storming stage you might need to refer to the 'ground rules' to highlight acceptable behaviour and prevent personal attack.
- You might encourage everyone to take on an individual responsibility in the norming stage, to help foster commitment and group cohesion.
- At the performing stage you can help maintain motivation through regular contact with others, recognition of effort and praise.
- At the adjourning stage you might suggest a group celebration to mark successful completion or an evaluation of the project in order to learn for the future.

DANGER!

Be aware that the time spent at each stage can vary enormously and that groups can return to earlier stages. For example, if individuals leave or join the group the dynamics may change, and the group may revert to storming or norming. Real life is frequently messier than the model might suggest!

INTERESTING FINDING

It's been suggested that just as individuals can participate in either 'surface' or 'deep' level learning so the same applies to group work. Yan and Kember (2004) found that some student groups tended to adopt the strategy of 'task' focused surface learning (motivated by wanting an 'easy life') while others used deeper learning (motivated by the desire for greater understanding). 'Surface' groups copied material, swapped notes and tended to revise together, while 'deep' groups discussed and shared ideas.

4. INTERACTIONS

The one thing that happens in all groups is that people interact with each other, and as sections 2 and 3 demonstrate, there is plenty of potential for misunderstandings and resentment in any group! The way that individual members interact and express themselves is influenced by previous group experiences, beliefs about group-work, cultural background and current personal circumstances in addition to role preferences.

TRY THIS

What are some of the things you can do to help ensure that interactions between individuals remain positive and constructive throughout a group project?

Our suggestions include:

Ground rules

Draw up a set of ground rules at the beginning of a group project. These will be rules that all members agree to adhere to and which might cover attitudes and values as well as actual behaviours. For example:

- Attend all meetings, and be on time.
- Contribute to the overall project, in the way agreed.
- Listen to each other's point of view.
- Respect each other's point of view.
- Offer positive feedback and focus on ideas not personalities.
- Raise any dissatisfaction in the group, before reporting it to outsiders.

This may sound very formal, and group members sometimes view this as a waste of time. So why take the time to do this? Agreed ground rules provide a 'safe' way of moderating behaviour, as negative behaviours can be raised and discussed in relation to the ground rules. They can save time in the long run.

Monitor behaviours

Give your 'teamworker' a break by monitoring:

Attendance issues

Are there any attendance behaviours that suggest the group is not functioning effectively? Does anyone consistently fail to turn up for group meetings or consistently fail to arrive on time? These may indicate that these people are, for whatever reason, not committed to the group. It is usually better to discuss such issues (respectfully) as they arise rather than risk unvoiced resentment.

Participation imbalance

Does everyone in the group participate in the discussion and decision-making? Not everyone needs to say the same amount, but if one member is dominating while another is staring out of the window, then the group may be experiencing problems. Kline (1998) emphasises that the quality of thinking within groups will reflect how members treat each other. She stresses the importance of listening with respect, treating everyone equally, honouring boundaries and giving everyone time to speak free from interruption.

Energy levels

Does the group appear energetic and motivated or are people slumped and looking bored? Is it time for a break? Is it time for a change of topic or a new discussion? Is it time to call it a day and set a new meeting date?

Group factions

Is there one cohesive group or several subgroups? Successful groups demonstrate interdependence, positive regard for all members and commitment to the shared goal.

Group discomfort

Try listening not only to what is being said but also to what is not. Are there any problems that everyone is aware of but nobody openly acknowledges? Group discomfort may be the result of one person not performing or not co-operating. Once again, the ground rules may help you raise this issue safely.

TOP TIP

When considering how well your group is working, try thinking about interactions at three different levels.

1. Firstly, consider the personal level. How are you interacting with the group? What are you contributing and offering?
2. Next, consider the interpersonal level. How do individuals within the group interact? Are there cliques or factions?
3. Then consider the whole-group level. Is everyone needed and is everyone playing a part in ensuring group success?

IT WORKED FOR ME

'The course I'm on involves a lot of group-work. At first it really annoyed me but then I realised that my negativity was making others feel uncomfortable. These days I make more effort to feel enthusiastic and I think more about the impact that I'm having on others in the group. Although I'd still prefer to work by myself, I actually quite enjoy project work now!'

5. ASSESSMENT

One of the challenges raised by project work is assessment. Some group projects may require you to rate your own performance, your peers' performance or both. Sometimes tutors award individual grades. Although each approach raises different considerations, all require unambiguous assessment guidelines that are applied consistently by everyone involved.

Self-assessment

Self-assessment removes you from the traditional 'learner' role and requires you to appraise your own performance objectively. Some advantages of self-assessed group work include:

- Knowing that you will subsequently be asked to assess your own contribution may increase your commitment to the project.
- It can enhance the dialogue between students and tutors and foster more productive meetings.
- Accurate self-assessment requires you to work out for yourself where you have performed well and where further improvements can be made.
- It provides an introduction to the type of appraisal procedures that are used in many work environments.

Effective self-assessment depends on high levels of self-awareness. Review the section on intrapersonal intelligence (page 49) and see chapter 12 for more on this.

INTERESTING FINDING

Contrary to what you might expect there is evidence that students can be accurate self-assessors, awarding grades that correlate with tutor grades (McDonald & Boud 2003, Stefani 1994).

Peer assessment

Peer assessment is frequently used in group situations, partly because students are considered better placed than tutors to evaluate individual contributions. Peer assessment may involve single or multiple assessors who may or may not be anonymous.

The perceived benefits of peer appraisal are that it promotes personal accountability and encourages each team member to participate. On the down side lies the danger that learners might use anonymous end-of-project appraisal to punish any slackers (even though this tactic does not bode well for future group experiences) or give overly generous face-to-face feedback (Brooks & Ammons 2003, Norcini 2003). Try doing the following in order to maximise the benefits of peer appraisal:

1. Don't wait until the end of a project before giving feedback to others. If there is a slacker in the group try to raise and discuss this problem early on. And never use 'anonymous' feedback at the end of the project as an excuse to 'get even'.
2. Check that there is a common understanding across your team members on how to apply the assessment criteria. Does this understanding match your tutor's expectations?
3. Consider carefully the language you use and how it might be interpreted.
4. Try to be fair and unbiased.
5. Do not do any 'deals' with fellow students!
6. Do not ignore areas where there could be improvement. Consider the words of Solon: 'In giving advice, seek to help, not please, your friend.'

LOOKING AHEAD

The ability to give and receive feedback without causing distress, and to listen and react objectively is a hugely valuable skill. Many people don't enjoy giving feedback because it makes them feel uncomfortable and a common workplace complaint is that managers don't provide enough feedback. As a group learner you have the opportunity to practise both giving and receiving feedback!

Tutor assessment

 Individual assignments are entirely your own work or at least they should be! In project assignments individual contributions may not be identifiable – even though every member is expected to have contributed. Tutor assessment raises questions about whether each person in the group receives the same grade or, if not, how are individual grades calculated?

Individually graded projects often include an element of 'built in' self-assessment such as:

• a reflective account of the project work and your own contributions
• a personal 'interview' to explore the project process and findings.

These are taken into account by the tutor when assessing.

INTERESTING FINDING

In a sample of 80 students Brindley and Scoffield (1998) found that over half viewed assessment as solely a tutor role.
What's your position? Why?

---

6. ONLINE GROUPS

We've discussed some issues that arise in face-to-face groups, yet this is not the only way of undertaking group work. Today many students and employees are involved with online or virtual groups and these pose some different benefits and challenges. What would you say these are?

Here are some of the benefits of working in an online group:

• There is time to consider carefully your response to postings or queries and because of this words can be selected more carefully than in speech.
• The physical appearance of team members cannot distract from the content of the postings.

- All postings and dialogue can be saved for later reference.
- People can work when it suits them and accommodate their own bio-rhythms.
- No travel issues (transport availability, travel time or costs).
- May better suit students with physical disabilities than more traditional modes of delivery.
- If well-facilitated, we have found that online environments encourage greater honesty, both in terms of self-disclosure and providing feedback to others.
- Online group work provides good preparation for many workplace environments.

And here are some of the challenges of online group work:

- Members of online groups may need IT skills and technical confidence.
- Projects intended for face-to-face groups may not have been well-adapted for online use.
- Communication can be particularly slow/frustrating if there are 'laggards' in the group.
- It is very easy to misinterpret the tone and intention of postings.
- Technology can fail!
- It takes longer to type than to talk, which may prevent full exposition of ideas.
- Students and tutors are not always adequately prepared for this style of working.
- There can be resistance if students are not used to this approach.
- Participants may feel isolated.

(Reed & Mitchell 2001, Hron & Friedrich 2003, Lockyer et al. 2001, Oliver & Omari 2001, McFadzean & McKenzie 2001.)

So what are the implications of these benefits and challenges?

Much of what we've said about group-work so far still applies but you need to consider these points in the context of virtual groups. Setting ground rules, for example, remains good practice, although you may want to include 'netiquette' or the 'online etiquette guide to good behaviour'.

Project sequencing, timings and individual activities must still be agreed but now you need to take into account the lack of face-to-face contact and possible asynchronous communications.

Group interactions should still be monitored. For example, is everyone in the group contributing? If not does this signal disinterest in the topic, a refusal to engage with the group, a period of considered thinking or something else entirely?

Salmon (2002) developed a five-stage model of online group development and believes that virtual groups progress through the five stages: initial access, early socialisation, information exchange, knowledge construction and broader knowledge application. The moderator's role is to facilitate this progression.

TOP TIP

If you are involved with an online group project our advice is:

- Embrace the technology and ask for technical support if you need it.
- Spend time on introductions and 'getting to know you' activities.
- Select your words very carefully – they may be all you have!
- If you write a response in a highly emotional state, always wait a while before you post it!
- Ask yourself whether the project raises any additional practical challenges that would not be found in a face-to-face setting.
- Let group members know in advance if you will be off-line for any period of time.
- Enjoy the opportunity it presents rather than grumbling that it is different!

7. INVOLVING OTHERS

In this chapter we've focused on how to work successfully in groups towards a common assignment. Yet there are probably many other people that you can involve in your study both formally and informally. Who else could contribute to your own learning success?

- parents?
- friends and siblings?
- partner?
- tutor or programme leader?
- employer?

How could they help you? Here are some of our ideas.

Parents/friends/partner/siblings could:
- proofread
- act as sounding boards for ideas
- critically appraise your work
- provide information
- provide emotional support
- offer practical help, e.g. cooking meals!
- act as role models
- pass on their experiences
- prevent interruptions, e.g. take phone messages.

Tutor/programme leader could:
- provide formal academic feedback
- help assess your strengths/weaknesses
- assist with topics that you are finding particularly tough
- provide additional academic support
- give advice on study skills/revision/examination technique
- provide information
- offer guidance on future options and how to fulfil them.

Employer could:
- provide feedback on your strengths/weaknesses in the workplace
- provide a character/work reference
- offer long-term career advice
- provide contacts and networking opportunities.

Success is rarely due to the efforts of one individual. Most successful people recognise the contribution of others around them – those in their direct team but also those in the wider groups. You probably have many people willing to support and help you. Why not let them?

TRY THIS

Draw up a list of six people and brainstorm the ways that they might help you with your learning.

What do you need to do to make this happen?

Are there also people that you can help?

IT WORKED FOR ME

'When my employer gave me the opportunity to study for an MBA I was determined to do well. I set the spare bedroom up as an office and set aside four evenings a week for study. The problem was that as soon as I shut the office door I shut my wife out. She felt increasingly excluded. It took us a while, but we finally found ways to share the experience, and our relationship is much stronger.

She now reads all my essays – I've realised that you don't have to be a subject expert to spot grammatical errors or an argument that doesn't make sense – and she also helps with my revision. I graduate in three months' time and we like to joke that it will be *our* MBA.'

SUMMARY

The mindmap on page 107 summarises the key terms in each section of the chapter. Take a look and see if you can recall the points that were raised by each.

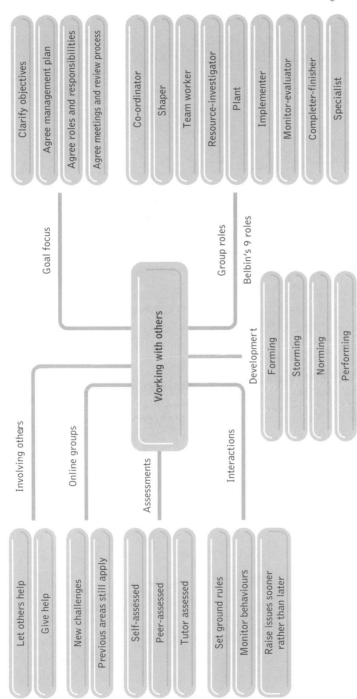

Figure 5.4 Working with others

6 Reading Techniques

KEY POINTS

- ☐ Effective readers clarify their purpose before beginning to read
- ☐ There are lots of different reading techniques
- ☐ This chapter looks at scanning, skimming, focussed reading, speed reading and quantum reading
- ☐ Effective readers can use a range of techniques
- ☐ Effective readers choose the most appropriate technique for their purpose

INTRODUCTION

Before you read the next paragraph, consider the following statement carefully, and decide whether you agree with it. *(Hint: this could be a trick question – so don't take it too seriously).*

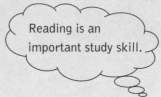

Reading is an important study skill.

We hope that you agree with the sentiment of the statement. (We believe it is overwhelmingly true that being able to read is important for most students on most courses. Pritchard et al., 1999). However, we asked the question in this way to see whether you picked up on the idea that reading is a **single** skill. We prefer to think of 'reading' as a generic description that includes many different kinds of reading activities.

Imagine someone told you that 'moving' is a single skill. Would you agree the same skills are needed for both running and dancing? We don't! If you want to be good at both running and dancing you need to develop both skill sets. The same is true for reading.

We believe that there is no such thing as a **single optimal** reading strategy. Winograd and Johnson (1987) suggested that most of the research around reading comprehension strategies was based on the **false** assumption that there is a single optimal reading strategy. The evidence supporting the value of different reading strategies is growing (Magliano et al. 1999, McCutchen et al. 1997, Lorch et al. 1993).

To be an effective and efficient reader, you'll need to master several different reading techniques and learn when to apply them. We've divided this chapter into six sections. The first section (below) helps you to clarify your purpose. The next three sections explore the three **key** reading techniques (scanning, page 111, skimming, page 113, and focused reading, page 114). The fifth section (page 117) covers speed reading and quantum reading, and the final section (page 126) looks at choosing the right technique for your purpose.

1. CLARIFY YOUR PURPOSE

Step 1. Before you do anything else, think about exactly what you're trying to do – in other words, **clarify your purpose**. This is an essential first step before deciding what you need to read and which type of reading strategy to employ.

There is a list of general questions in the activity below which you can use to help you to clarify your purpose for most reading assignments:

TRY THIS:
PRE-READING ACTIVITY

1. **What do I need to know?**
   - What do I already know about the topic?
   - Why do I want more information?

- How do I want to extend my knowledge?
- Where are my information gaps?

2. Where can I find the information?
- Is the information source readily available (e.g. reading list)
- Do I need to select a book from several choices?
- Do I need to do a literature search?
- Do I need primary or secondary sources?
- Are my Information Literacy skills up to the task? (see 'Top Tip' below).

3. What, *exactly*, do I want from this material?
- Find a specific fact or figure
- Identify a person's point of view on a particular subject
- To clarify a particular concept
- Evaluate the evidence for a particular point of view.

4. How quickly can I find what I need?
- How important is the task?
- How much time do I have?
- How much time do I want to give?

5. Will I need to recall the information in future?
- If so – what actions will I take to help my recall?
  (See also chapters on note-taking and memory.)

TOP TIP

We recommend that you learn how to conduct effective literature searches. It's a key skill which we touched on in chapter 3. Most colleges and universities offer courses and tutorials for developing online searching skills. Why not have a word with your tutors or librarian and see what's available?

2. SCANNING

When you don't have a lot of time, and you need to find a specific piece of information fast, try 'scanning'. Usually, you'll have a clear sense of purpose and can identify the key word or words very easily.

When you begin your scan, rather than reading every word, simply move your eyes over the content very quickly, trying to locate keywords. Once you find a keyword, stop and read the sentence or paragraph around it. If this meets your needs, don't read or scan any more. If it doesn't meet your needs, continue to scan the rest of the content.

We 'filter out' most of our incoming sensory information, so most of it never enters our consciousness. But when something is important, we tend to notice it. Have you ever noticed how you can suddenly hear your name in a crowded room, even though there might be dozens of conversations going on at the same time? Because our name is important to us, our filtering system lets this through.

Scanning for information works well when you know what it is you're looking for. In other words, you need to have a clear focus. This may be a person's name, or a number or date, or even a location. The clearer your focus, the more successful your scan is likely to be.

TRY THESE ABC ACTIVITIES NOW

A Focus: We receive a lot of sensory information, and our 'focus' helps us decide what to pay attention to. This is equally true when we're driving, shopping and skim reading. We tend to notice information that is relevant. So it's really helpful to take a few moments and be explicit about your focus *before* you start to skim read.

Give yourself three minutes to look around the room now and notice all the red items in the room. Once your time is up, turn to the end of this chapter for your next instructions (page 129).

B Scanning: Now turn to pages 24–6, and see how quickly you can find how many hours it takes without sleep before there's a significant reduction in cognitive performance.

Think about and reflect on your experience (if you're not a natural reflector, see chapter 3):

* Were you surprised by your time?
* How easy did you find it to 'scan' the material without reading for content?
* When you found the figure (18.25 hours) did you read the whole sentence for meaning?
* Did you stop as soon as you found the information, or did you continue to scan?

C Scanning for dates: Now, try scanning this nonsense text below. There are three dates (month and year). See how quickly you can locate them.

Ghst bnretiu tthxucp thref ffghfgh mkiul se wdartvcx os pqqmwk xosle mn m daoo yej dilc dishtenavy hio awia nuct dc, zi jcm-skdiokmcd nj. Th slkd co dksk Nov 1997 sdf mkoi ploi ju mxmxnc. E asi uw sdm. Lpoti thso SHDH bnbi jsbr upi yjpihjy ehst, ohjy nr dsuomh? Mpy s htrsy vpfr.

Nfmspof iio Slitzer Nizel w djka ewpll aqw. Lospd e djdiusd thjid oikjasd nxjzo mwnaq, maksp djdjj wewpqilr. Pod sdn bhfj thjd ejlakjsdn nvifcpidf sadenflkzjxc, ekfjhksdilklwesdf jkdk sa a kdiof wmwopd klwwpef.

iio Slitzer Nizel Nfmspof w djka ewpll aqw. Lospd e thjid oikjasd mwnaq, maksp djdjj wewpqilr. Pod sdn bhfj thjd ejlakjsdn nvifcpidf, ekfjhksdilklwesdf jkdk sa a kdiof wmwopd. w djka ewpll aqw. Lospd e djdiusd thjid oikjasd nxjzo mwnaq, maksp djdjj wewpqilr. Podfg Feb 2004 sdn bhfj thjd ejlakjsdn nvifcpidf sadenflkzjxc, ekfjhksdilklwesdf jkdk sa a kdiof wmwopd klwwpef. Bndh sioam etho mkji stad jfuic bnwiao shmkru thsoppd hehhweid thklpoi iloi s kk k sldofdu nd iuhe gs. Xnzenuj nej n qwodsi thaos, wnkjo mksiau ensmd. O jduisut njdu asy egwiudh ghajks koodld:

Dfnrmfk mkopfdivo ythjrlef m dnj mskl. Ndkosidsd md as pl dp asmkwed huiuiu. Mosidkosd May 1899, Msdae ea, e as, lpoeouqq bbeuy nu as oi zxm kO

Did you find this easier or harder then the previous example? Why do you think that was so? Usually people find that if the information they are looking for contrasts with most of the information surrounding it, then it's quicker and easier to pick out.

You may realise that you're already an accomplished scanner, and scan for all types of information without thinking about it. If you don't, it's easy to practice. Why not try scanning nutrition labels for information on salt content, or newspaper articles for references to global warming.

3. SKIMMING

When you want to gain a high-level overview of the reading material, try 'skimming'. This technique is helpful to give you a feel for the overall content. It's *not* about collecting in-depth information.

To use your study time effectively, you need to learn how to choose what to read as well as what not to read. Given that you can sometimes 'skim' a book in 10–15 minutes, this can save you a lot of time compared to reading every word.

If you're not already a 'skilled skimmer', think of it as a two-step process.

Step 1. Preparation
Step 2. Preview

Step 1 Preparation

What are you going to focus on? You may use keywords, just as you would for 'scanning', but usually when you're skimming, your focus will be slightly broader. For example, rather than using the author's name, your focus may be to uncover another perspective around a particular issue, or you may want to see how extensively a particular topic is covered.

Step 2 Preview

Think back to before you began reading this book. Did you skim through it? If you picked it from a bookshelf, did you 'flick' through the pages?

With a bit of practice, you can 'skim' many books in 10–15 minutes, and you can 'gut' a book in less than an hour. 'Gutting' usually involves reading the first and last sentences in addition to the list below.

- foreword
- table of contents
- headings and sub-headings
- first and last paragraphs in each chapter
- tables and graphics.

As you skim, take a note of any sections you might want to revisit with a more focused approach (see next section).

Have you noticed how long the titles are in scientific research papers?

Yes. Most are 10–20 words! Sometimes I only read the title before deciding whether or not to read the rest of the article.

4. FOCUSED READING

The best way to gain an in-depth understanding of most written material is to follow the four steps in the 'Reading Staircase', shown in figure 6.1 (pages 115 and 116). The first step applies to all the reading techniques, the second step applies to 'skimming', and the third and fourth steps are specifically important for focused reading.

The two most important points to take away are:

1   You need to 'actively process' the text in some way.
2   You need to read the text several times (Maloney 2003).

Asking lots of questions (see Table 6.2) is probably the most common way to engage in 'active processing', but there are other methods. Note that many of the note-taking tips from chapter 8 also apply here! If the text is very dull, try bringing a little humour to it. If you like to visualise, imagine attending a lecture . . . how could the presenter make the key point in a way you would never forget?

Table 6.2 Different types of questions

	Relevance	Prediction	Challenge	Fact/Opinion	Associate	Explain
How can I apply this to x?						
Where's the author going with this?						
How do we know this is true?						
What are the other possible explanations?						
What do we know since this was published?						
What is the author going to conclude?						
How reliable is the evidence?						
What evidence supports the claim?						
Where else was this presented?						
How would I explain this to x?						

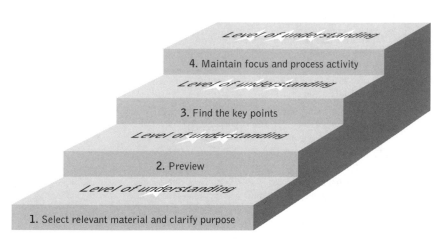

Figure 6.1 The focused reading staircase

Step 1: Select relevant material and clarify purpose

Selecting the relevant material and clarifying your purpose is important for all of the reading techniques and strategies covered in this chapter – but as focused reading takes a lot time, make sure you get this step right!

What information do I need?

Step 2: Preview

In the previous section we discussed how to skim or preview material. This second step in the 'focused reading staircase' is important for two reasons: a) it helps you make sure that the content is relevant and is worth an investment of your time and b) previewing helps to build context, and this has been shown to be important for improving recall and comprehension. (McWhorter 1998, Taylor et al. 1995).

Is this the best source of information?

Step 3: Find the key points

The third step, finding the key points, can be a bit tricky sometimes. You need to be able to 'pull out' and summarise the key messages.

What is the author actually saying?

You may have noticed that we start each of our chapters with a list of key points. Do you find them helpful? Do you agree with the ones we've chosen? (it's OK if you choose different points – it's your reading experience ☺)

Many academic texts are very dense, written in the passive tense with long words. In other words, they make the reader work hard for the information. Often the key points turn out to be relatively straightforward, but sometimes they may be implied, rather than stated explicitly, and then you need to read between the lines and ask yourself 'What is the author implying by this?'

A good comprehension test is to see how easily you can explain the key points to someone else.

Step 4: Maintain focus and process actively

Having identified the key points, you now need to 'drill down' and actively process the information at a more detailed level. The best way of doing this is by asking yourself lots of questions.

What do I think about . . . ?

In Table 6.2 we've listed some of our favourite questions for active processing. They fall into a number of different categories, for example predicting what will come next, distinguishing between fact and opinion, and challenging assumptions.

See if you can complete Table 6.2. Note that some questions fall under more than one category. (Answers on page 260).

Figure 6.1 *(cont'd)*

IT WORKED FOR ME

'I used to find most text books very boring to read, and spent hours staring blankly at the pages, hoping the information would somehow go into my brain. Then I read about using metaphors. So now when my concentration lapses, I try to come up with a metaphor that works in context. It's really fun. My inner dialogue might go something like this:

> *The author's argument is like. . . . a football game. Before you make the team selection you need to look at everyone's form and gather the evidence. The team captain is like xxx, which stands out as high profile and different from the rest of the team. There are lots of different training strategies which represent the such-and-such schools of thought . . .*

I really like thinking in metaphors and I use the technique to liven up all kinds of reading material.'

5. SPEED READING

The promise of being able to read a complete book in 20 minutes may capture our imagination, but the reality of many speed-reading techniques leaves many of us disappointed. Do you think the problem lies with the techniques, or could it be the way we execute them?

Anne Jones, five times winner of the World Speed Reading Championships and winner of six gold medals at the Mind Sports Olympiad, reads more than 2,000 words a minute and remembers enough information to answer detailed questions with remarkable accuracy. In contrast, it is alleged that Woody Allen, after taking a speed-reading class and reading Tolstoy's *War and Peace*, was asked what the book was about and replied 'Russia.' And there lies the dilemma for most of us – how can we increase our reading speed without reducing our comprehension and recall?

Surprisingly, there is very little reliable evidence around reading speeds in relation to comprehension. The good news is that speed readers (800–1,800 words per minute) seem able to *summarise* the main points just as accurately as 'normal readers' (250–320 words per minute), but their *detailed* comprehension and recall is not quite as good (Just & Carpenter, 1987).

We think there are some interesting questions that may challenge some of our assumptions about reading. If you're curious about your own reading speed, why not time how long it takes you to read the following story, and we'll help you estimate your reading speed at the end. If you want an accurate assessment, don't stop to try the exercises – but do come back to them *after* you've finished the story.

So . . . when you're sitting comfortably, we'll begin. . . . *Many years from now, in a galaxy far away, over 800 hot orderly bodies filed into a vast auditorium. Outwardly, their physical shapes were cosmically varied, but their earnest faces and pristine uniforms (issued only the night before) easily identified them as the new academy recruits.*

Xenoky, a young man of noble origins, twitched his many stalked eyes to search for a friendly face. Yarine, a slightly built Sivapithicine caught his primary eyes. They exchanged a warm smile, took their seats together and waited attentively.

Once everyone was seated, the presentation began. Most of it was good inspirational stuff. Pretty much the same stuff that had been presented at the beginning of every year since the academy opened. And after an hour the same weighty manual was handed out for the delegates to read. Everyone was given 15 minutes to read through it.

Nervously, Xenoky leaned over to Yarine, seeking confirmation that he had indeed mis-heard the instructions. In hushed tones he whispered to his colleague: "Was that 15 or 50 minutes we have?" Yarine smiled. "15," he said, and deftly opened the heavily bound manuscript.

For Xenoky the next 15 minutes evaporated. He had just finished the first chapter when they called time. Up until that moment, he had regarded himself as an excellent reader. How was it that the other students had been able to read the entire manual in such a short time?

Yarine sensed his companion's discomfort, and invited him for an Earth Latte after the presentation. It didn't take long before the conversation turned to reading speeds.

"So, tell me, Xenoky, how did you learn to read?"

"Hmm, that's an interesting question. Well, I knew my alphabet from a young age, and was taught how to 'sound out' each word phonetically. Then really it was just a matter of practice. Of course, as I improved I recognised whole words instantly . . . but basically it was a phonetic approach."

"How, exactly, did you make the transition to silent reading?"

"Mmmm. I'm not sure it was really a transition. From what I recall, once my teacher was happy with my reading accuracy, she encouraged me to 'read in my head' . . . using the same process, but just not saying the words out loud. What about you?"

"Well, my experience started off much the same as yours. But my people regard reading alone in your head, or subvocalising, as a pre-requisite for the next level of reading. If you say the words silently in your head, it really slows down your processing speed. I understand that for most sentient beings, this is limited to about 350 words per minute. That's probably why you didn't make it to the end of the first chapter of the manual. For me, I was taught to trust my eyes before reading with my ears became a habit."

"Wow. That's amazing. Do you think you could teach me to read like you do?"

"Sure. The thing to remember is that sometimes I still read like you do. What's important is to be able to match your reading strategy to the context."

"How do you mean?"

"Well, sometimes you need to subvocalise, or read the words in your head. Poetry is a classic example. A small percentage of our children lose the ability to hear the words in their head, and they can't ever appreciate the full richness or beauty of the classical poets. It's very sad."

Yarine paused, looking very distant for that split moment. Then his expression changed, and he continued, "It's very important to consider how you're going to use the information you're reading. If I need to follow complex or subtle arguments, I use your reading method. But if I just need to store information, like in a manual, then speed reading is great. Let me show you something."

Yarine opened a lazer pen and scribbled on one of the drink mats. When he'd finished he handed the mat over to Xenoky. "Here. See how many words you can read on either side of the plus while keeping your reading eye focused in the middle."

Eagerly, Xenoky took the mat from his friend.
It read:

recruit	+	star fleet academy
find safe	+	always trust
departure time	+	canteen tray
and everywhere	+	include nonsense
random span	+	enjoy being
when you	+	design a

After a few moments, Xenoky burst out laughing. "Gosh, that's harder than it looks. How would this help my reading speed?"

"Well," replied Yarine, "using the 'trusting your eyes' approach, you need a broad peripheral field of vision. So, with each moment of focus, you take in as much information around it as you can. Doing exercises like this one for a few minutes each day can really help you improve your peripheral focus. Aim to take in a whole line of information, keeping your eye focused in the centre of the line. I'm able to read three lines at a time now."

"I'm impressed," conceded Xenoky generously. "Any other tips?"

"Sure. Here's another basic drill we use at school. Let's use the security codes listed in chapter 7." Yarine reached over to retrieve Xenoky's drink mat and began scribbling intently. As he handed the mat back, he explained "This time you cover up the codes, then flash the first code to yourself for half a second or so, then write down what you remember. This doesn't give you time to say the words to yourself, so you have to rely on your visual memory. It's a great way to break the subvocalising habit. I usually remember 10 digits with a 0.25 second exposure. Go on, give it a go!"

Xenoky flashed the first code to himself, and frowned as he wrote down '47p'. He also remembered the 4-digit codes, but struggled with some of the longer ones. His friend encouraged him, "It's hard at first, but again if you practise a few minutes each day, you'll be surprised how quickly you improve.'

"Yes, I can see how this will help. It's fantastic. Thanks Yarine. I'll soon be speed reading like you."

"Well, this is only the next step for us. When our children can speed read at 1,000 words per minute, we teach them 'quantum reading'. It's a fundamentally different approach which allows us to absorb written material at speeds of 20,000 to 30,000 words per minute."

"Are you kidding?"

"Absolutely not. It's a core skill for all our secondary students. It's not really reading in the way that you think of it, as you don't focus on the words at all. Its more about letting the unconscious aspects of our brain download all the 'visual input' without filtering, and then accessing the information without being consciously aware of having learned the material."

"Do you think it will work for me?"

"Should do, if your brain functions are similar enough to mine. Do you agree that we are constantly bombarded with huge amounts of sensory information, mostly visual and auditory?"

"I guess so."

". . . and because there is a limit to how much stuff we can pay attention to at any one time, our subconscious filters out most of this sensory input, so only a small amount of the information is ever processed consciously. Have you noticed that once you've decided to buy a new auto-spacer, you suddenly 'see' them all over the place?"

"Yes, it happened when I bought my Telstar V8. They're quite unusual, but I saw at least a dozen others like it in the following week."

"Well, they were there before, its just that your subconscious filtered them out. If you've experienced the phenomenon, it suggests to me that your brain is similar enough to mine in that it only processes a small amount of the available sensory input in a conscious way. Which is great, because that means the 'quantum reading' techniques probably will work for you. Would you like to try a short experiment to find out?"

"Absolutely."

"Well, if you have time now, come back to my room and we can try one of the diagnostic tests we use to check the readiness of our students for this technique. I need to find a suitable book. We find it works best using one of the antique paperback dictionaries."

"So what do I have to do?"

"Well, I'll ask you to hold the book 12–15 inches from your face. It'll help if you close all your extra pairs of eyes, and just use your primary pair."

"No problem."

"*Now the hardest part is that you need to focus about 6–9 inches behind the book. This seems really counter-intuitive, but you mustn't focus on the words, or you'll end up processing the information consciously, and that defeats the whole purpose. It may take a little while to get used to, and the first time I tried it made me feel a bit dizzy.*"

"*That's OK. I'll be fine. What then?*"

"*Well, keeping the focus behind the book, you turn over each page, at a rate of about one per second. When you get to the end, turn the dictionary upside down and flick through the pages again at the same rate. This shouldn't take more than about 10 minutes. When you've finished, you'll give me the dictionary, and I'll flick through and randomly pick some words. For each word I choose, you then guess whether the word appears on the right or left page, which column, and whether it's at the top or bottom.*

"*Sometimes it helps to agree a marking grid before hand. Then you can just call out the number. The first time I tried this exercise, I was absolutely stunned by the results. Even though I felt dizzy, I was 80 per cent correct – which is way, way above chance. It convinced me that we have usable information that was stored unconsciously – and that's the basis for 'quantum reading'. Are you ready?*"

"*You bet. This is going to be great.*"

Table 6.3 Guide to your reading speed

Time	Approximate Reading Speed	Comments
Less than 1 minute	1,600 wpm	Outstanding
2–3 minutes	480–1,000 wpm	Excellent. It seems that you're already a proficient speed reader
4–5 minutes	310–480 wpm	Good. Your average reading speed is quite high for 'normal' reading
5–7 minutes	230–310 wpm	Average. This is typical of higher education students who are reading normally in their native language
More than 7 minutes	< 230 wpm	Slow. Improving your reading will really help your study efficiency

So how long did it take you to read the story? To estimate your average reading speed in words per minute (wpm), all you need to do is divide 1,640 (the number of words in the story) by the number of minutes it took to read (rounded to the nearest minute). See Table 6.3 for a guide to interpreting your result.

Were you reading at your normal speed, or did you speed up, to see how fast you can read? Or perhaps you read this slower than you would read study material because you were enjoying the story. No one is suggesting that you apply speed reading techniques to your leisure reading.

As we said in the introduction, speed reading seems to work well if you need a high-level overview, perhaps to produce a written outline or summary. If you read at 1,000 wpm rather than 250 wpm, you quarter your reading time. How useful would you find that? And as mentioned in the story, 'quantum' reading is a fundamentally different approach to reading altogether. There is very little hard evidence, but the theory is intriguing and there's lots of anecdotal evidence from people who have mastered the technique.

Why not try some of the tips and techniques mentioned in the story and in the rest of this chapter? But remember if the arguments presented are quite subtle, and you need to follow them carefully, you'd probably be better reading in a focused way, as discussed in the previous section. Building on the point we made earlier, be careful to choose the reading strategy that most suits your purpose!

Here are our four Top Tips for Faster Reading!

TOP TIP 1 *Don't Subvocalise*

Most people read for life at the speed which they learned when reading aloud. The brain can process information much more quickly than that. If you can make the switch to reading without hearing every word in your head, it will dramatically affect your reading rate.

TOP TIP 2 *Use a Pacer*

Typically, when we read, our eyes make rather jerky movements and 'back skip' quite frequently. This slows you down. If you run your finger or a pencil underneath the words as you read, it's possible to increase your reading speed just by increasing the speed you move your finger. It may feel unnatural at first, but many students report quite dramatic improvements using this technique, which was pioneered by Evelyn Wood in 1958.

TRY THIS

Ask a friend to follow an imaginary circle, about 3 metres in diameter, and watch their eye movements. Now ask them to follow your finger as you draw an imaginary circle in the air, and compare how their eyes move. Did you notice a difference in how smooth or jerky their eye movements were?

You should notice that eye movements are smoother when they are following a finger or pencil. Without a pacer to follow, the eyes move like they are following a series of dots, and may even back-pace!

TOP TIP 3 *Reduce the Number of Fixation points per page*

One of the main differences between 'normal reading' and 'speed reading' is the number of 'fixations' your eyes make on a page. Instead of fixing on every word or two, experienced speed readers are able to read a page with as few as six 'fixations' (see figure 6.2). Practically, this is the main difference between the two reading techniques.

To be a successful speed reader, you have to learn to infer connections between those segments of the text that you've sampled (Just & Carpenter 1987), and to take in more information at each fixation point. The letter recognition and visual-peripheral vision exercises in the story are designed to help you do this, and both have been shown to have a positive effect on reading speed (Chung et al. 2004).

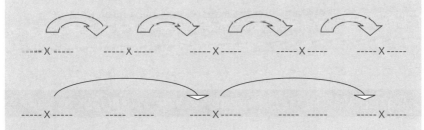

Figure 6.2 Eye fixation points per page

TOP TIP 4 *Adjust Your PC*

You may be surprised to know that the visual properties of text and background affect your reading speed on a computer screen. In a recent study involving undergraduate students, Wu & Yuan (2003) found that the colour, lightness and brightness of the foreground, relative to the background, affect the average reading speed. From their findings, they recommend that to improve your reading speed when using a computer screen:

- the foreground should be darker and the background should be lighter
- the foreground colour should be less saturated than the background colour.

And interestingly, while the optimal settings for speed were frequently found to be in conflict with visual preferences, Wu & Yuan (2003) reported they were unable to locate any literature discussing the relationship between visual preference and reading speed.

6. MATCHING THE TECHNIQUE TO THE PURPOSE

You should now be comfortable with the differences between the reading techniques we've discussed. However, it is not enough simply to know about them. You have to know when to use them (Lorch et al. 1993).

So for example, you might know *how* to scan or skim a text, but this isn't the same as knowing *when* it's the best approach to use and *why*. And this brings us back rather neatly to the importance of knowing your purpose, and being clear about why you're reading in the first place.

TRY THIS

Circle the technique you would use for each of the following tasks:

1. I need to confirm the percentage of smokers under the age of 25.
    Scan   Skim   Focus

2. I'm going on a field trip to China next month and want to buy a travel guide. There are three books on the shelf, and I don't know which one to choose.
    Scan   Skim   Focus

3. I need to prepare a 90-minute presentation explaining this author's main ideas.
    Scan   Skim   Focus

4. I've been asked to critique this research article.
    Scan   Skim   Focus

5. I'm trying to decide whether to take this course next semester. The material for each week is based on a different chapter from this textbook.
    Scan   Skim   Focus

6. I'm revising for my exams, and need to check what year a particular study was published.
    Scan   Skim   Focus

Answers on page 261

Q. *How can I use this right now in my study?*

Take a few minutes to think about why you're reading this book and jot down your ideas. Here are some questions you might like to ask yourself.

*   How much time do I have for this task?
*   How important is the outcome to me?
*   Am I being assessed on the content? If so, when, and how?

- Would I use different strategies if the assessment was soon, rather than at some future unspecified time?
- What is my interest in the material?
- What is my emotional involvement?

QUESTIONS AND ANSWERS

Q. Do you have any tips for choosing the best book from a reading list?
A. There are lots of things you might take into consideration, including:

- What do you know about the author?
- Who is the intended audience (e.g. undergraduate students, postgraduate students, experts, the general public)?
- What do you already know about the topic?
- What are you supposed to know before you read the book?
- Do you like the structure, style and layout?
- Do you like the use (or absence) of visuals, tables and graphics?
- Has the book been recommended, and by whom?
- Does the book look interesting?
- How well does it cover the areas you're interested in?

Q. Can I apply these reading strategies on my e-learning course?
A. Unfortunately, a lot of e-learning courses are not particularly well designed from the learner's point of view. Often the navigation forces you to work through each page in sequence and so it can be very difficult to scan or skim the material.

We suggest you ask to preview the material before signing up – and see how you feel working through their sample content. If you can't preview the material, ask how their designs cater for different reading strategies. When enough people start asking, the designs will change!! (And also be aware that although almost all e-learning designers *say* they cater to different learning styles, this often means no more than including audio files.)

Q. My friends and I received an email, claiming that:

'Aoccdrnig to rsceearh at an elingsh uinervtisy, it deosn't mttaer in waht oredr the ltteers in a wrod are, the olny iprmoatnt tihng is taht the frist and lsat ltteer is in the rghit pclae. The rset can be a toatl mses and you can sitll raed it wouthit graet porbelm. Tihs is bcuseae we do not raed ervey lteter by itslef but the wrod as a wlohe.'

Is this true?

A. No, what this e-mail suggests is probably an urban legend. It claims we can read the text because the brain recognises words as a whole, but Edinburgh scientists, Dr Richard Shillcock and Dr Padraig Monaghan, have evidence that reading actually involves splitting words in two. Although the position of the first letter does help with word recognition, the brain has to recognise both halves of the word.

Reading a couple of scrambled sentences might not seem too hard, but most of us would soon tire of the extra effort required, according to Martin Turner of the Dyslexia Institute. (T. Radford, the *Guardian* 25 Sept. 2003)

SUMMARY

This chapter is summarised in figure 6.3 (overleaf).

TRY THIS

(continued from page 111)
If you're curious why focus is important, try this activity now.

You've just spent three minutes noticing all the red items in the room, now read on . . .

Close your eyes and give yourself 60 seconds to recall all the *green* items in the room.

How easy or hard did you find it? Do you think it might have been easier if you'd focused on green items at the beginning of the exercise?

We receive a lot of sensory information, and our 'focus' helps us decide what to pay attention to. The same applies when we skim read. We tend to notice information that is relevant. So spend a moment thinking explicitly about your focus *before* you start to skim read.

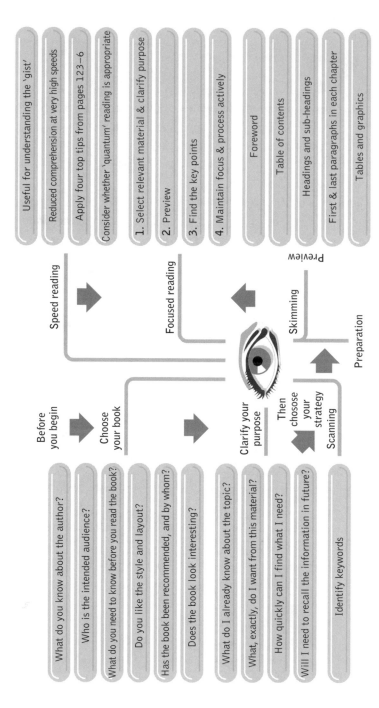

Figure 6.3   Summary of chapter 6

7 How to Remember Everything You Need To!

KEY POINTS

☐ Educational success requires accurate recall

☐ Luckily, there is no such thing as a 'bad memory'

☐ Accurate recall involves focus, encoding and retrieval

☐ There are many techniques and activities that can help you to remember

INTRODUCTION

In this chapter we look at how to remember information.

Most educational programmes place a high value on accurate recall. Although the increasing use of continuous assessment, open-book exams, problem-based learning and project-based assignments may indicate a move away from an 'over-reliance' on memory (Ryan 2003) the need for accurate recall will not disappear. The ability to recall information precisely can also save you time and energy outside the learning environment.

This chapter looks firstly at how you remember and the implications this has for your study. We then describe some specific techniques and activities that will help you remember.

How do I remember?

Various models of memory have been proposed. Although some controversy continues, most people agree that it's useful to consider three distinct memory systems: sensory, short-term and long-term memory. These are shown in figure 7.1 below. This model has some implications for learning.

Here's our list. You may be able to think of others.

- Memory is a process or an activity; it is not a noun.
- You must focus on information before it will enter your short-term memory.
- You must encode or process the information before it is stored in long-term memory.
- In order to recall information you must 'locate' then 'retrieve' it.

Sensory memory
Sensory information enters from the environment
May be considered as 'perception' rather than 'memory'
Most sensory input is thought to be immediately lost

1. Focusing

Short-term memory (STM)
A temporary store with limited capacity
Involved in conscious thought
Processed/manipulated information is transferred to Long-term Memory
STM is involved with retrieval from LTM?

2. Encoding   **3.** Retrieving

Long-term memory (LTM)
A permanent memory store
LTM includes episodic and semantic memory
(Episodic = memory for events/incidents
Semantic = memory for facts and knowledge)

Figure 7.1   A model of memory

- The more deeply and richly you can process or encode information the easier it will be to remember that information accurately and easily.
- There are techniques to help you focus, encode and retrieve so that you will remember more effectively and efficiently.

INTERESTING FACT

Taxi drivers have different brains! London black-cab taxi drivers have larger hippocampi than other people, as a result of memorising the roads and routes through London – a compulsory part of their training (Maguire et al. 2000).

Making the model work for you

The model in figure 7.1 shows that in order to remember something you must first focus on it properly.

Although focus is indeed essential, we also know that certain types of information are more likely to be remembered.

If you make sure that you always understand your learning material and then process it as deeply and vividly as possible you are more likely to remember it. Most of the memory techniques below involve focus and encoding. In addition, material that is particularly vivid, unusual or humorous is also likely to be better remembered because it 'attracts your attention' (Schmidt 1994).

TRY THIS

Ask yourself the following questions to see how well you focus.

	Always	Usually	Sometimes	Occasionally	Never
How often are you *unable* to say what you have read after studying an article or set reading?	☐	☐	☐	☐	☐
How often do you engage in 'simultaneous' activities, such as watching television, when studying?	☐	☐	☐	☐	☐
How often do you find yourself copying passively from set texts?	☐	☐	☐	☐	☐
How often do you find yourself thinking about other things when studying e.g. plans for the evening?	☐	☐	☐	☐	☐
How often do you find yourself distracted by external events – noises, friends – when studying?	☐	☐	☐	☐	☐
How often do you nod off while studying?	☐	☐	☐	☐	☐
How often are you holding a mental dialogue with the author when reading?	☐	☐	☐	☐	☐

How did you do? If you answered 'never' or 'occasionally' to each question except the last (for which the desired answer is 'always'!) then congratulate yourself. If you scored less well, you might want to look at Chapter 2 'Preparing for Study'. This contains suggestions on how to improve your focus through maintaining good physical and mental states and a conducive study environment.

TRY THIS

Read through the following list of words.

Shampoo	Parrot
House	Chair
Sky	Measles
Baker	Beach
Clock	Purse

Now cover the page and write down all the words you can remember.

You have probably remembered more words from the start and the end of the list than from the middle. This is called the 'primacy' and 'recency' effect. By dividing your study activity into small units you can maximise the amount of material you recall simply by increasing the number of 'starts' and 'ends'.

Now, try the same exercise using the following list of words:

Schampnera	Papegoja
Hus	Stol
Himmel	Massling
Bagare	Plage
Ur	Papper

How many words did you recall this time? We are guessing not many, unless you are fluent in Swedish! It is difficult to process information unless it is meaningful. Have you ever tried to memorise information without fully understanding it first? What happened?

How comprehensive is the model?

Q. *I understand the model but does it really account for everything I learn?
    What about things like playing the piano or learning to drive? Surely we
    learn these differently?*

A. That's a really good question, and yes, different types of memory have
    been proposed. The model above only shows semantic memory (memory
    for facts and information) and episodic memory (memory for personal
    events). 'Procedural memory' is the phrase used to describe the acqui-
    sition of skills such as typing or driving and it differs from semantic
    and episodic. It is possible for someone to have episodic amnesia, for
    example, yet retain the skills that they have learnt earlier in life.

INTERESTING FACT

Although you cannot learn new information while asleep the good news
is that processing and consolidation of previously reviewed material does
take place during sleep, indicating the wisdom of saying 'I'd like to sleep
on it' (Wagner et al. 2004).

How to remember more accurately

From the model and activities presented above, it should be clear that
improving your memory is all about improving your focus, encoding and retrieval
skills. There are various techniques and activities that can help you do this.
Here we will consider:

- **M**nemonic techniques
- **R**epetition
- **C**hunking
- **O**verlearning
- **M**eaningfulness
- **I**nterference
- **C**alm state

Mnemonic techniques tend to be most useful for learning information that must be learnt 'word perfect' yet has little inherent organisation or meaning — lists of names or digits. They are less useful for material that has intrinsic meaning or where your recall should be faithful to an original account but not word perfect, e.g. summarising a theory.

MNEMONIC TECHNIQUES

As with many new tools, you may find that it takes a little practice before you are comfortable or proficient at using the techniques included here. Try not to let this put you off and remember that you may not want to try or use all of them. Decide which are best suited to your learning needs and then practise them.

Acronyms and acrostics (leading letters)

Definition: An acronym is a word or term developed from the first letter of each to-be-remembered item. An acrostic is a complete sentence, or a series of words, in which the first letter of each stands for one of the to-be-remembered items.

Examples: My Darling Aunt Sally is one acrostic for remembering the order of mathematical processes, multiply, divide, add then subtract. In medicine it is even possible to purchase a textbook of medical mnemonics! (Khan 2003). The acronym 'Mr Comic' could be used to remember the techniques included in this chapter.

Use: Acronyms and acrostics are useful for memorising information that must be recalled in a specific order. In addition the letters provide 'clues' that facilitate successful recall since solving one clue should help you to solve the others. (See below and page 138.)

Rinse Out Your Grandmother's Boots In Vinegar – colours of the rainbow: **r**ed, **o**range, **y**ellow **g**reen, **b**lue, **i**ndigo and **v**iolet

My Very Easy Method Just Speeds Up Naming Planets – **M**ercury, **V**enus, **E**arth, **M**ars, **J**upiter, **S**aturn, **U**ranus, **N**eptune and **P**luto

HOMES – **H**uron, **O**ntario, **M**ichigan, **E**rie and **S**uperior (Great Lakes)

Fat Cats Prefer Mice Very Well Fried – **F**at, **C**arbohydrate, **P**rotein, **M**inerals, **V**itamins, **W**ater and **F**ibre (food groups)

KILLS! **K**idneys, **I**ntestines, **L**ungs, **L**iver, **S**kin (excretory organs)

King Philip Cooked One Gorgeous Steak – **K**ingdom, **P**hylum, **C**lass, **O**rder, **G**enus and **S**pecies (biological categories)

Rhymes

Definition: Self-explanatory? A rhyme or rhythm that helps you recall the to-be-remembered items.

Examples: Many adults cannot remember the number of days in each month without chanting the rhyme that begins '30 days hath September'.

Use: Rhymes help ensure accurate order recall and act as a memory cue. They are easier to recall than non-rhyming sentences (Rubin & Wallace 1989). By inventing your own rhymes you necessarily have to focus and encode the material, and the rhyme itself provides retrieval clues.

Memory pegs

Definition: Here, you learn each to-be-remembered item by associating it with a previously memorised noun. Since each noun represents a number you can then remember lists in order.

Examples: First of all you need to learn your 10 nouns or 'pegwords'. These are usually words that rhyme with the numbers one to ten, such as:

| 1 – Bun | 2 – Shoe | 3 – Tree | 4 – Door | 5 – Hive |
| 6 – Sticks | 7 – Heaven | 8 – Plate | 9 – Wine | 10 – Hen |

Pegwords can also be words that look like the numbers, for example, swan for number two or six for spoon. Whichever you choose you need to thoroughly learn and visualise each pegword. For example, is yours an iced bun or a fruit bun? Is it round?

Let's imagine that you are studying different energy types including wind, wave, biomass, geothermal, solar and fuel-cell technology. Your memory peg for wind could be an image of yourself standing on a giant iced bun hanging grimly on to a wind turbine while struggling not to be blown away by a gale. Next you might imagine your shoe full of water with seaweed hanging out of it. For biomass you might picture your tree emerging out of a giant bonfire formed from timber waste. The trick is to visualise a clearly defined and ideally bizarre image for each.

Use: One advantage of using memory pegs is that if you do forget an item, it will be clear where your memory has failed. Memory pegs also allow you to retrieve an item directly without working through the entire sequence. By adding additional detail to your mental pictures you can remember not only a list of terms, but also some additional facts around them.

IT WORKED FOR ME

'I found the visualisation techniques difficult to apply to abstract terms, so now I tend to keep these techniques for my personal life – for remembering shopping lists for example. Instead I've found it more useful to learn specialised abstract terms by developing my own acronyms or acrostics.'

TRY THIS

Some people believe they are not good at visualising or that it is in someway childish. Yet there are situations when most of us visualise, for example when planning a journey or making household purchases. Do you try to picture the roads or the colour of your décor in these situations?

Imagine that someone asks you for directions to the nearest hospital. How would you respond?

Verbal directions are often based on landmarks that we see in our 'mind's eye', such as traffic lights, pubs or garages rather than street names. If you use visualisation in situations like this, then you can also use it in your study.

And, coincidentally, the next mnemonic builds on this idea of giving directions. . . .

TOP TIP

So far we have described visualisation as a mechanism for learning. Yet it can also be used to change state. Athletes, for example, may visualise themselves winning events as part of their mental preparation. This generates feelings of success, confidence and motivation rather than the negative state that could result if they dwelt on 'worst fears'. You can use visualisation to change your state prior to beginning study or before exams.

Loci techniques – rooms and journeys

Definition: These two memory aids are the oldest known and both involve placing the to-be-remembered items into a visualised known location. Before you can use these techniques you must memorise a room or journey. This initial investment of time is not wasted since the room or journey can be used for future memory tasks. You can also extend either by including more rooms or by making the journey longer.

To use the 'room' technique, firstly select a room well known to you. Next, mentally walk around the room and select a number of locations that fall into a natural order. For example, logical locations in your kitchen might be the sink, rubbish bin, windowsill, fridge, kettle, microwave and oven. To remember a list of items you mentally walk around your room and place one to-be-remembered item in each location.

With the journey method you visualise a very familiar journey – walking from your home to a local shop, for example – and select 'drop off' points along the way. You then mentally place one to-be-remembered object at each of these points. Position them carefully and note their location, size, shape and colour. You need to visualise them as vividly as possible, so make the images funny, sexy or plain extraordinary, ready to grab your attention when you revisit the location!

Examples: The original Loci example dates from 500 BC. Simonides left a banquet hall to take a message, when the roof collapsed crushing everyone inside. The bodies were too badly damaged to be identified so Simonides recalled where each person had been sitting and subsequently deduced that memory can be improved by relating items to locations.

Use: You can use Loci techniques whenever you have a list of items to remember. Although rooms and journeys are typically used in these techniques, any variation on this is possible. Once again these techniques help you remember items in order.

TOP TIP

You can use Simonides' example whenever you are attending events, such as meetings or seminars, where you do not know the other participants. Quickly sketch out the seating plan and as people introduce themselves write each persons name by their location. You can then use this plan to memorise names and faces.

IT WORKED FOR ME

'I make notes on different parts of the page and try to remember the layout. I've found this works well as a memory jogger. For example, when I was learning about planets, stars and moons I wrote my notes in three separate columns using different colours. Visualising this later helped me to recall the information.'

TOP TIP

It is often easier to remember country-specific information by writing on a sketch map rather than by making linear notes. The progress of a war, for example, can be learnt by writing notes and arrows on a map rather using long-hand notes.

Associations

Definition: You form an association every time you link to-be-remembered information to another image or event in a meaningful way.

Examples: Stalactites hang from the ceiling and the word contains the letter 'c'. Stalagmites build up from the ground and contain the letter 'g'. Similarly, a Bactrian camel has two humps as seen in the initial letter B and a Dromedary camel has one as in the letter D. Associations can be idiosyncratic. Louise's son remembers that kidneys contain 'Bowman capsules' by thinking of a teacher called Mrs Bowman.

Metaphor or analogy is a form of association frequently used in teaching. For example, the concept of homeostasis is often taught using the analogy of a thermostat. Memory pegs are specific examples of forming associations.

Use: The more associations you can make between new and existing knowledge, the easier it is to remember, since you are increasing the total number of mental 'cross references'. As Leonardo da Vinci wrote: 'In some way everything connects with everything else.' You simply have to find the connections!

You can also associate activities with learning. For example, you could decide to rehearse the periodic table whenever you wash up. After a little while this behaviour will become automatic.

Stories

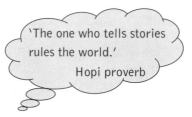

'The one who tells stories rules the world.'

Hopi proverb

Definition: In this technique you incorporate the to-be-remembered items into a story.

Examples: Just as rich story-telling was important in pre-literate cultures for transmitting knowledge, so the same technique can be used today. Here is a story for remembering Shakespeare comedies. Are you sitting comfortably? Then I'll begin. . . .

My tale begins in on a cold wintry day (A Winter's Tale) *when two rich Italian businessmen decided to move from Verona to England* (Two Gentlemen of Verona). *They moved to Windsor, where they quickly met and fell in love with two beautiful laughing women. The weddings made these two women so happy that they laughed more than ever before* (The Merry Wives of Windsor).

Both wives fell pregnant straight away and nine months later, in the middle of a summer night (A Midsummer Night's Dream) *the women woke up and found themselves in labour. The labours were extremely long and painful but their husbands said that they were making much fuss about nothing* (Much Ado About Nothing). *Then on the twelfth night of labour* (Twelfth Night) *everything seemed to get worse!!*

Even though the babies were still not born two Italian relatives arrived. These were a merchant from Venice (The Merchant of Venice) *and his wife. She was a lovely woman, despite the rumours that at one time she had been a real shrew* (The Taming of the Shrew).

As they all sat waiting in the hospital the weather broke and an almighty storm took place (The Tempest). *So much seemed to be going wrong it was* *almost funny (*Comedy of Errors*). At last the labours were over and the babies were born (*Love's Labours Lost*) and they were identical in weight and measurement (*Measure for Measure*). Everyone was so relieved that things had turned out all right. "All's well that ends well," said one husband (*All's Well that Ends Well*). "From now on you can have whatever you like," promised the second (*As You Like It*).*

This story offers the titles of 14 of Shakespeare's comedies. The other three all have proper names as the title and these can either be incorporated into the story as the names of characters or remembered separately. The names are Cymbeline, Pericles Prince of Tyre, and Troilus and Cressida.

Use: It is important that your story has a clear thread or plot and is meaningful for you. You would probably want to personalise the story shown here and it is also important to try and use all your senses and imagination. Story mnemonics offer a very simple way to memorise information and have been shown to be effective (Hill et al. 1991). Unlike some of the other mnemonics described there are no logical clues if you do forget part of your story.

TRY THIS

Think about the different mnemonic techniques we've talked about.

Which are particularly attractive to you? Is that because they suit your intelligences or preferred learning styles? Or do they lend themselves to your particular studies?

Keyword mnemonics

Definition: This is a very specific mnemonic used when learning a foreign language. To develop keywords you combine two mental images. The first is an image of what the word sounds like, which is combined with an image of what the word means.

Examples: 'Maison', the French word for house (pronounced maze-on) could be remembered using an image of a maze on top of a house.

Use: This technique can be used when learning foreign language vocabulary.

DANGER!

Remember that most mnemonics help you to learn by rote. Learning all the facial nerves or a list of alkali metals does not demonstrate a depth of understanding. View mnemonics as memory joggers and recognise their limitations! Despite this health warning there is little doubt that accurate memorisation is a prerequisite to achieving success in formal study.

REPETITION

We tend to forget the bulk of what we are studying very quickly, although the subsequent rate of loss slows down. Therefore it makes sense to return to material quite soon after it has first been studied, and then allow gradually longer intervals between each repetition or review (Buzan 2003). As always, the material should be fully understood since repetition alone cannot add depth to your knowledge. It may take several cycles of review before material is fully committed to long-term memory but once you are confident that you have 'learnt' a subject area then quick reviews of the material are all that is likely to be needed in future.

CHUNKING

How many words did you remember from the two earlier lists? In a classic article published in 1956, G. A. Miller proposed that the number of items we hold in our short-term memory is seven, plus or minus two.

However, the more 'information' contained within each item, the more information you hold overall. Increasing the amount of information within each item is called **chunking**.

Overleaf is an example of 'chunked' energy sources:

Full list	Chunked list
Wind generation	**Renewable energy sources:**
Hydro power	Wind generation
Tidal power	Solar power
Biomass	Tidal power
Geothermal energy	Hydro power
Solar power	Geothermal energy
Coal	Energy from waste
Oil	Biomass
Gas	
Energy from waste	**Non-renewable energy sources:**
Nuclear energy	Oil
	Natural gas
	Coal
	Nuclear energy

Learning material is often already 'chunked' when presented. For example, individual elements are grouped within the periodic table, diseases may be chunked into different therapy areas, and geographical concepts might be chunked under physical, social or economic geography.

Experimenting with different ways of chunking will not only help you condense the information but you will also find new connections between information, which by itself means deeper processing and better recall.

Acronyms are another example of chunking; single words or phrases like 'Mr Comic' take you to detailed information.

TRY THIS

Think about one of the subjects that you are currently studying. How is information chunked in those subjects? And what chunking strategies have you developed yourself?

For example, in media studies films may be categorised under different genre such as comedy, thriller, romance, or film noir. However, you may have also developed your own ways of rembembering films, by chunking according to director, year of release, nationality, leading actors etc.

OVER-LEARNING

Have you ever spent the night before an exam cramming? This is a high-risk learning strategy. Last-minute cramming raises the risk that information will not be retrieved since it has only been superficially studied. Six months later there may be little you can spontaneously recall.

Over-learning through repeated review leads to faster and better recall of information. Think of the phrase 'etched on my mind' and try to over-learn the material that you need. You can over-learn using many different techniques – repeated review, chatting with friends, reading notes, through mindmaps etc. Again, the more active your learning the better it will be!!

MEANINGFULNESS

Your brain tries to add meaning to all situations – and this includes all new information. Most of the memory techniques presented in this chapter are about adding extra layers of 'meaning' and 'organisation' to material. Both classic and recent memory experiments have demonstrated that it's easier to remember material when it you find it meaningful and interesting (Miller and Selfridge 1950, Shirey and Reynolds 1988).

Since material is stored in many ways, the more richly or 'deeply' you can process information the more retrieval cues are at your disposal.

TRY THIS

Many of us know someone who can recall every football fixture and score for the past umpteen seasons, or who can rattle off the names of Oscar-winning films together with their starring actors and actresses.

What facts have you learnt purely because they are interesting and meaningful to you? How did you learn them and how much effort was involved?

Now ask other 'trivia experts' how they remember their facts and note down all the different ways.

You are likely to find that trivia experts do not work hard at trying to learn facts; they absorb them through personal interest and connecting new information with old.

INTERFERENCE

New information can interfere with, or 'get in the way' of previously learnt information. Did the lists that you tried to learn earlier interfere with each other? The more similar the different sets of to-be-remembered material, the greater the capacity for interference.

The implications for study are:

- Take breaks between topics or try to space them out.
- Try to avoid learning similar information 'back to back', unless the two are related. It is best not to learn Latin vocabulary followed by French vocabulary, as there may be interference. Instead follow the Latin with an entirely different subject, such as maths, and save French revision for later (Higbee 1996).

CALM STATE

The relationship between our emotional state and ability to perform well is discussed in chapter 2, Preparing for Study. Can you think of a time when you have been 'put on the spot' and not been able to recall a crucial piece of information or even think of anything to say? Excessive anxiety or stress makes it more difficult to remember accurately.

Although it has been suggested that highly emotional or arousing incidents – such as where and how people heard of the death of Princess Diana or the events of 9/11 – are well remembered, recent evidence suggests this is not the case. Instead, self-perceived accuracy is higher, probably due to rehearsal via conversations with others and 'mental replays' (Talarico & Rubin 2003).

Some arousal *is* needed for successful learning and you should aim for a heady mix of relaxation plus alertness. Cassaday et al. (2002) found that recall of words was better when study took place in relaxing rather than a neutral environment.

RETRIEVAL

Many of the techniques described in this chapter help you to retrieve information by either providing contextual clues or signalling when you have forgotten something. There are some other techniques that also help you retrieve information when you need it.

When trying to remember information make use of the fact that your brain organises and cross references information in many different ways. Memory experiments have shown that even when people find it difficult to retrieve 'known' vocabulary, for example, they can still identify the number of syllables or the initial letter at better than chance rates (Brown & McNeil 1966). Next time you have forgotten something try working your way through the alphabet, or think about the length of the word to see if this aids recall.

Similarly, have you ever struggled and failed to recall an important piece of information, only to find that it pops into your head sometime later when you are no longer directly thinking about it? Higbee (1996) advises 'thinking around' when trying to recall information, by mentally trawling through

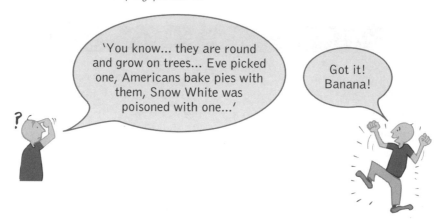

all your associations with that item. When trying to attach a month or year to an historical event, for example, consider what else you know about that event. What came afterwards? Was there a subsequent coronation or peace agreement that might help you place the date? What preceded the event? Even thinking about when the event was taught within your curriculum might help you remember the correct date. These may lead to greater success than frustratingly focusing on the forgotten date.

FORGETTING

There are several theories of why we forget, including the following.

Fading: This theory states that memories simply fade away. There is limited supporting evidence for this, but if memories do fade the implications for learning are clear – over-learn and review.

Interference: This was described above and refers to new material 'getting in the way' of old.

Retrieval difficulty: This theory suggests that we never lose memories but sometimes we can't access them, and has emerged from physiological evidence in which brain stimulation has awakened 'forgotten' memories.

When acquiring new information you may 'learn and forget' several times before you really know the material. Continue to 'process' and 'review' until you are able to retrieve the information easily and accurately.

TRY THIS

Write down all the capital cities you can recall and put the list in an envelope.

Repeat this tomorrow and compare the list. Is it the same? Are there any additions or omissions?

Any changes demonstrate that we may know more about a topic than we retrieve at any one time. One practical application is, where possible, to give yourself time to retrieve information when studying.

EXTERNAL RESOURCES

This chapter has focused on techniques and strategies to help you remember but there are also external resources that you can use. What resources do you use to help you remember? Our list included:

- IT and software resources e.g. task lists, reminders
- diary
- other people
- watch alarms
- post-it notes
- whiteboards/chalkboards
- address/telephone books
- mobile phone reminders.

There is no reason not to use external aids. Successful learning is partly about making smart choices.

LOOKING AHEAD

If you want to keep your memory in good working order you need to exercise it and use it regularly! Many of the techniques covered in this chapter are shown to be as effective for older people as they are for younger (Verhaeghen et al. 1992). It also seems that older people may optimise their learning by capitalising on their wider experience and enhanced skill set. Older people, it seems, may plan cognitive tasks more effectively than younger, by looking further ahead and making better use of external aids such as diaries or 'to do' lists (Maylor 1990).

SUMMARY

1. To remember successfully you need to **focus**, **encode and retrieve**.

2. Memory is not equivalent to understanding – although they are related.

3. The best way to learn is by making the material interesting, stimulating and relevant.

4. Strategies and techniques to help you remember include:

   - **M**nemonic techniques
   - **R**epetition
   - **C**hunking
   - **O**ver-learning
   - **M**eaningfulness
   - **I**nterference
   - **C**alm state

8 *Making Notes*

KEY POINTS

☐   Making notes helps you to organise your material, your thoughts and your learning

☐   There are several different ways of making notes

☐   Different skills are required for making notes in lectures and making notes from books

☐   Review your notes regularly and store carefully

INTRODUCTION

Why make notes? Note-making helps us to manage information and is an important skill, which should not be left to chance. A good set of notes will help you in your studies whereas poor notes may only confuse or mislead.

Many of the general points made about active learning in the chapters on memory and critical thinking also apply here.

In this chapter we look at:

•   What makes a good set of notes?
•   Different note-making techniques
•   Making notes in lectures

- Making notes from texts
- Selecting the appropriate technique
- Storing notes.

WHAT MAKES A GOOD SET OF NOTES?

You may have heard notes described as 'bare bones' that you later 'flesh out'. It's a useful metaphor since bones demonstrate many of the qualities of good notes (see figure 8.1).

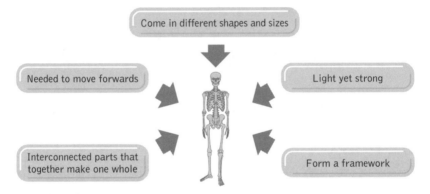

Figure 8.1 Notes as 'bare bones'

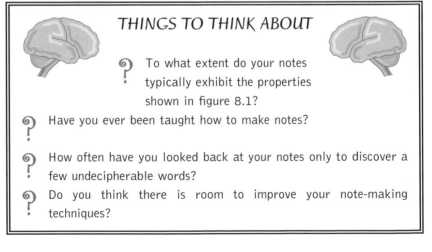

THINGS TO THINK ABOUT

To what extent do your notes typically exhibit the properties shown in figure 8.1?

Have you ever been taught how to make notes?

How often have you looked back at your notes only to discover a few undecipherable words?

Do you think there is room to improve your note-making techniques?

DANGER!

Imagine being given a pile of bones and asked to build the skeleton. Unless you know something about the animal this could be an impossible challenge. Yet learners sometimes borrow other people's notes, even when the topic is new to them. What's more, notes are often idiosyncratic and may include non-standard abbreviations or personal comments that are not meaningful to others. If you do borrow notes bear these potential pitfalls in mind!

DIFFERENT NOTE-MAKING TECHNIQUES

There are several different note-making techniques. Some particularly suit specific contexts or material, or you may have personal preferences, perhaps relating to your preferred intelligences and learning styles (chapters 3 and 4).

TRY THIS

What note-making techniques do you generally use?
What note-making techniques are you aware of?
Which note-making techniques have you tried?
How useful were they?
Why?

Now take a look at the mindmap in figure 8.2 on page 156 – it shows some common approaches to note-making.

How do the techniques shown here compare with your own list?

Don't worry if your own list is shorter. Our experience suggests that many learners rely on one or two techniques.

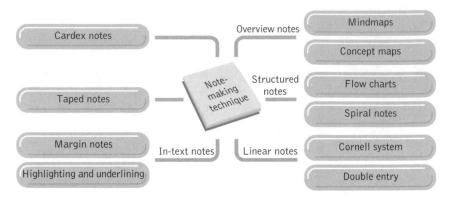

Figure 8.2 Different note-making techniques

Concept maps and mindmaps

If you were making notes from this book we hope you would see that, although different topics are covered in individual chapters, they are all interconnected. Perhaps we should have produced this book as a gigantic mindmap, since this approach makes the 'big' picture highly visible?

Concept maps and mindmaps, which are very similar, allow you to see the big picture. Mindmaps are usually attributed to Tony Buzan (1993) and concept maps to J. D. Novak (1990). The differences are subtle although mindmaps typically show one central concept and concept maps show idea networks.

To make a mindmap hold your writing pad landscape and write the topic heading in the centre or heart of the page. Draw the main arteries coming out of this and write the key concepts alongside. Let each of these divide into smaller veins and write secondary ideas. Be as creative as you wish and experiment with colour, acronyms, symbols and pictures.

If this approach is new it may initially feel alien, particularly if you're used to linear techniques. Mapping may hold more instant appeal if you prefer to focus on the big overview rather than on detail, or if you prefer visual images to text (see chapter 4). Don't use this as an excuse, though – remember that learning styles should be viewed as current preferences and not used as a barrier to development or experimentation.

What advantages do you think mind mapping offers?

Seeing the big picture is one advantage offered by mindmapping. Others include:

- Flexible order allows you to insert branches where you wish.
- You can easily show associations between branches using arrows.
- Masses of information can be presented without overload.
- You can join individual mindmaps together to see the MUCH bigger picture.
- It is easy to return and add additional notes.
- Mindmaps offer high visual appeal.
- They promote creativity.
- They can be undertaken as a group activity.

TRY THIS

If this approach is new to you try rewriting your latest notes as a mindmap. How do the two techniques compare?

LOOKING AHEAD

 Many work-based activities also require good note-making skills, including:

- taking official minutes at meetings
- client meetings
- reading, digesting and summarising reports or documents
- interviewing
- internet searching
- telephone conversations.

Perhaps we should consider note-making a life skill rather than an academic skill?

Spiral notes

Circular processes (including, for example, biological and chemical cycles and many business practices) can be summarised in spiral diagrams (see figure 8.3).

It is always worth considering if new information is a disguised circular process.

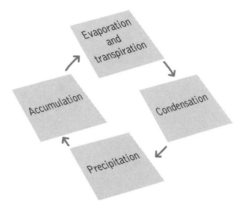

Figure 8.3 The rain cycle: An example of spiral notes

Flow charts

Flow charts are commonly used in business to chart complex processes involving choice points. You can adapt this technique to summarise other processes or proceedings such as the path of historical events or the plots of films or literature. How might you summarise the course of World War II as a flow chart? Could you summarise any of your learning topics in this way? Figure 8.4 shows a method of using flow charts.

Matrix notes

The matrix system is a structured approach used to make comparisons between categories of information. It is hugely useful, since many academic courses require learners to compare, contrast and evaluate. See figure 8.5 for an example.

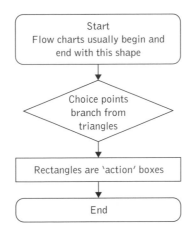

Figure 8.4   How to use flow charts

	Insulin	Anti-diurctic hormone	Thyroxin	Cholecystokinin
Produced by	Pancreas beta cells	Hypothalamus via posterior pituitary	Thyroid gland	Duodenal mucosa
Purpose	Lower blood glucose concentration	Stimulates water re-absorption	Stimulates metabolism and growth	Stimulates release of bile
Target organ/cells	General	Kidney	General	Gallbladder
Symptoms of under production	Hunger, thirst and excessive urination	Excessive urine production and thirst	Dry skin, weight gain, lethargy, breathlessness,	Malabsorption syndromes
Symptoms of over production				
Control mechanisms				
Hormone antagonist				

Figure 8.5   Example of matrix notes comparing hormones

One benefit offered by a matrix system is that the items of interest are compared across the same dimensions. In some cases you will need to identify the dimensions yourself before completing the grid, an activity that may itself take considerable time and thought. For example, psychology students making notes on Skinner, Freud, Piaget and Maslow might need to generate their own list of comparative dimensions such as key concepts, model of man, research methods and areas of application.

TRY THIS

How might you use the matrix method to summarise key differences between influential people in your own discipline?

Linear notes: Cornell notes

Pauk (2000) devised the Cornell technique. Here you divide the page vertically leaving a couple of inches blank across the bottom:

Recall cues	Main notes
Right & left columns	In the right-hand column you record in paragraph form, notes which contain the key ideas. When you have finished you read the right-hand column and add 'key words' or 'cues' to the left column.
Recall aloud	Read the cues and recall out loud (using your own language) the points made in the right column. Think critically about what you have learnt. Write a summary at the bottom the page. Help your learning by regularly returning to the cue words and vocalising your understandings.
6R	The Cornell approach is also called the 6Rs. The Rs are record, reduce, recite, reflect, review and recapitulation.

In the space at the bottom you write a brief summary or overview of the whole page – the 'recapitulation'.

Linear notes: Double-entry notes

Double-entry notes use a similar technique. Here you draw a line down the centre of the page:

Summary notes are then made on the left-hand side of the page and these include the key concepts, theories, facts etc. On the right-hand side of the page you raise key questions, insights, and evaluations. These may be added immediately, or later when you have had a chance to review your notes.	How does this differ from Cornell note-making? Is this approach better for note-making from books or from lectures? It's a bit like an ongoing debate. Is it useful for those times when I'm finding it hard to stay focused?

MAKING NOTES IN LECTURES

So far we've reviewed different note-making techniques. You should also consider whether you are making notes in a lecture or from a written text.

It is often more difficult to make good notes in a lecture, and some of the challenges presented by lectures include:

- You need to listen, think and write simultaneously.
- You have limited influence over the pace of the lecture.
- You cannot choose your teachers or lecturers.
- You are working alongside others and must respect their needs too.
- There may be external distractions.

However, the content of your notes should be absolutely relevant to your course.

TRY THIS

There are things that you can do to help make meaningful notes in lectures.

How often do you do each of the activities below, before, during and after a lecture?

Before the lecture?

	Never	Sometimes	Always
Arrive prepared: know the topic the lecture will address and how it fits into the course.			
Do any required preparatory work.			
Consider the type of material likely to be covered and which note-making technique you will use.			
Have a heavy session the night before . . .!			

Life is much easier when you arrive at lectures without a thumping headache and knowing which module you are attending! If you complete the preparatory work you should gain more from the lecture and be better placed to ask questions.

During the lecture?

	Never	Sometimes	Always
Track the stages of the lecture carefully – most presenters follow the 'say what they are going to say', 'say it' then 'say it again' format.			
Listen for clues on what is important – phrases such as 'The main idea', 'Never forget' and 'The most important thing'.			
Focus on the content and not the style of delivery.			
Ask the lecturer to pause while you capture key points . . .			

The introduction and the conclusion usually capture the *essential* ideas, so arrive on time, listen carefully and try to follow the arguments. Try to pick out only the important aspects but don't be afraid to ask the lecturer to slow down or present visual information for longer, while you do this. Chances are that if you haven't captured ideas you won't be the only one. Focusing on the content means you are less likely to become sidetracked by the funny or irritating mannerisms shown by either lecturer or peers!

After the lecture?

	Never	Sometimes	Always
Review and organise notes as soon as possible.			
Use other resources to fill in any gaps.			

Aim to read your notes after the lecture and clarify them where necessary. Although you may want to add to or amend your notes, see if you can do this without re-writing. Then use your notes and the course materials to guide your next study steps.

How did you rate?

What did you learn from your ratings? Is there one area – either before, during or after the lecture – which has greatest scope for improvement? Or is there room for small changes across the entire process?

Lectures can pose further challenges for learners who are not studying in their native language. Mulligan and Kirkpatrick (2000) found that overseas students may be disadvantaged by not easily recognising cultural cues (such as the gestures that may accompany important points) or differentiating between jokes and asides and important content. Their study showed that such students tended to focus more on pre- and post-lecture activity.

Students with specific needs or physical disabilities may also find it more difficult to make effective notes in lectures. It is difficult to give general advice because so much depends on the nature of the need or disability. Deafness or dyslexia present very different challenges. If you have any learning needs then let your lecturers know how they can help you.

Although this section has focused on lectures, some of the suggestions apply if you are making notes from television programmes, video or audio tapes. In some instances, though, you may have the luxury of replay!

TOP TIP

There is evidence that lectures with accompanying handouts are more effective learning tools than lectures alone. Perhaps you can ask your teacher for help with this? (Morrison et al. 2002, Austin et al. 2004.)

DANGER!

Remember that you are trying to make notes in a lecture, not produce a verbatim transcript! Some learners try to take down everything (Sutherland et al. 2002) even though effective note-making techniques are about summarising the key ideas and principal points.

IT WORKED FOR ME

'*I'm studying in the UK and my first language is Chinese. Even now, in the final year of my degree, I find that some lectures are too fast. I try to do some reading before the lecture starts, to try and get ahead and I always sit in the front row where there are fewer distractions. I've also asked to record some lectures so that I can listen to them again.*'

Although personal shorthand can be used whenever you make notes, one big advantage is that it saves you time and so it is particularly useful in lectures. It doesn't matter how idiosyncratic your shorthand is, providing that you can always make sense of it. Try to be consistent in any shorthand that you develop, so that you are not struggling to interpret it later.

TRY THIS

- Develop your own shorthand for words and concepts that you will use regularly
- Use international symbols and abbreviations for example:

use	for
<	less than
>	more than
+ve	positive
−ve	negative
inc.	increasing
stat^n	station
abb^n	abbreviation

- Use the latest text messaging abbreviations

MAKING NOTES FROM TEXT

Note-making from books raises different challenges. Here are some of our Dos and Don'ts for note-making from a text:

DO

- know the purpose of your reading (see chapter 6)
- check that you understand what you are writing
- decide on the best note-making strategy
- write full reference details and page number if you decide to include a direct quote in your notes.

DON'T

- overuse highlighting or underlining
- make too many notes
- write reams in longhand
- place yourself in danger of inadvertently plagiarising material by copying
- make notes while doing other things e.g. one eye on the TV.

Can you think of any others that you want to add?

IT WORKED FOR ME

'Early on I decided to study my course the easy way. I do two things without fail. I turn up to every lecture and I focus my attention on those texts flagged as 'essential reading'. I make good notes from both and check constantly that I understand the ideas. It's about being organised really – the hardest part is getting myself out of bed in the morning.'

Selecting the appropriate technique

We have introduced a number of different note-making techniques. In order to produce the most effective notes we suggest that you view every note-making situation as a problem to be solved (see figure 8.6). Approaching every note-making situation in this way will help you to consciously consider the options.

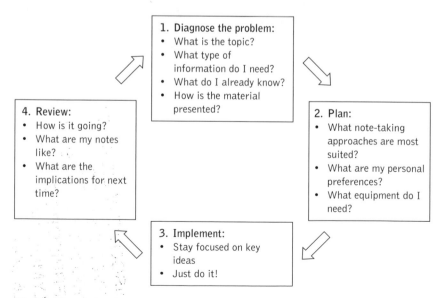

Figure 8.6 Classic problem-solving cycle applied to note-making

IT WORKED FOR ME

'I only use three styles of note-making and I think of them as the tools of my trade. I choose the most appropriate tool before starting any work. Sometimes I stick to one and sometimes I combine them – it depends on the subject and what I think will work best, but I always make a conscious choice.'

STORING NOTES

Figure 8.7 suggests how you might be able to make your notes more accessible and easier to review. There are also other ways of storing notes, including:

* Audiotape your notes and listen when travelling, jogging etc.
* Use a Cardex system to keep track of books and articles that you have read. Simply enter full reference details at the top of a card. Then write a sentence or key words to remind you of the content and indicate how useful you found it.

Figure 8.7 Making notes accessible

IT WORKED FOR ME

'I used to take notes on loose-leaf paper and then not bother reading them until I had an essay to write. I wasted so much time hunting down those scraps of paper. Now I empty my bag and file my notes every evening. It's saved me many "I know I've got it somewhere" moments.'

Making associations

When reviewing your notes don't forget to look for associations or relationships *within* and *between* topics.

Imagine, for example, that you are studying glass recycling. Within this topic you might compare local, national and international practices. You might also make between-topic associations by contrasting these with other 'environmentally friendly' practices such as recycling paper or using alternative fuels.

TOP TIP

Note-making techniques are changing with advances in IT and software. As handwriting- and voice-recognition software becomes more available, electronic note-making is likely to increase. This should make it easier to experiment with different forms. Worth keeping an eye on?

QUESTIONS FOR US

Q. *I usually copy out my notes many times. Are you saying I don't need to do that?*

A. You don't need to spend hours endlessly copying notes in the manner of 'parrot learning'. Think about the subject and what you need to know and understand. Think about patterns, themes and associations in the material. Think about the arguments presented, any advantages or limitations, questions raised, underlying assumption or values. Then make notes that are clear and meaningful to you. Review your notes regularly to confirm your understanding.

Q. *But surely this approach involves more work than simply copying notes out?*

A. Think of it as a high-interest monthly savings account. Although you must open an account and set up a standing order, the pay-off is far higher than if your money is kept under the mattress. It's about working smarter not harder – so a little time invested up front in good note-making techniques pays off when you get to the exams.

Q. *I've taken notes in the same way for years so why should I try to change?*

A. If you are actively processing information and your approach works then you may not need to change, although there may be ways to improve your approach further. Do you colour-code, for example? Remember that pictures can be included even on linear notes. Or you can insert mindmaps or flow diagrams into more traditional formats.

Q. *What do you think about making notes in books – I usually go through books with a highlighter.*

A. Be careful that you are actively processing the information – it's very easy to highlight or underline without really thinking. Also, you may subsequently read the same book for a different purpose, so beware if your highlighting is permanent.

Q. *I enjoy lectures and seminars but can't discipline myself to knuckle down and work on my notes afterwards – any suggestions?*

A. Ask yourself if your note-making activity always needs to be solitary. If you really prefer working with others you can work on mindmaps and flow charts in groups – perhaps at the end of each day following lectures? You still need to make sure that your time is well used. If your problem is poor motivation take another look at preparing for study (chapter 2).

SUMMARY

Note-making is about capturing key ideas in the best way, to help you manage information and learn efficiently. When preparing to make notes consider both the topic and the medium (lecture or text) before selecting the most appropriate technique. When reviewing and storing notes, always look for associations between topics.

9 Generating ideas

KEY POINTS

☐   It is easy to become stuck in particular ways of thinking

☐   Learners who can consider information from different perspectives are advantaged, since this is a key aspect of becoming a critical thinker

☐   We outline here seven techniques to help you view topics in new ways

INTRODUCTION

If you've ever spent time with small children then you've probably noticed the number of questions that they ask. What holds the sky up? Why does Granny have wrinkles? Why is there war?

Have you been able to answer such questions satisfactorily? Children often ask questions that you may not have considered before and that stimulate new insights.

Such questioning tends to subside with age. Why is that? Perhaps our environment becomes familiar and is not approached with the same curiosity? Or does it stem from the introduction to formal education, with its emphasis on rules and regulations? DeBono (1986) suggests that much formal education emphasises the skill of sorting information (categorising, comparing and contrasting) rather than generating information. Perhaps we cannot develop fully as learners if we continually bring the same thinking to a situation?

Einstein attributed his achievements to his questioning approach, saying: 'I have no special talents, I am only passionately curious'.

So how can you see things from all angles? How can you think about things differently? In this chapter we look at seven techniques intended to help you do this. The techniques outlined here should help you to engage in critical thinking (see chapter 10) since the ability to consider information from different perspectives is a precursor for becoming a successful critical thinker.

LOOKING AHEAD

 New employees sometimes display questioning behaviours similar to young children. They are keen to understand why things happen as they do, or why the organisation is run in a particular way. You may not always have answers in these situations either, but it is worth listening to the questions! New employees or new members see things with 'fresh eyes' and they can draw your attention to features that you now take for granted and which can be improved.

THE ICEBERG METAPHOR

You can use the iceberg metaphor to remind yourself why you should try to 'see things differently'. This metaphor says that the subjects you choose to study are like icebergs. Can you think of ways this could be true?

We think the subjects you study are like icebergs because:

- You probably begin most new programmes of study with some pre-existing knowledge or beliefs about the subject. This pre-existing knowledge can be likened to the very tip of the iceberg – it's visible and you are probably aware of it.
- Probably most of the topic will be new and unknown to you. This unknown element can be likened to the submerged part of the iceberg.

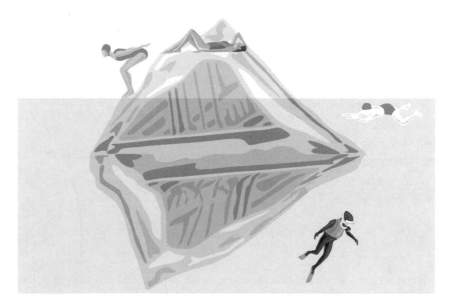

Figure 9.1   Different views of an iceberg

- Some aspects will be easier to reach and navigate.
- As with many icebergs there is scope to investigate previously unexplored facets and make new discoveries.
- The subject is evolving and changing, just as icebergs do not remain static in size or shape.
- There are many different ways that you can experience your subject, depending on the direction you approach it! The people in figure 9.1 will all have a very different view!

Exploring the iceberg

When you are first getting to grips with a topic you need to acquire information (see chapters 6 on reading and 10 on critical thinking) in order to gain an understanding of the topic. If you rely on a single text you run the risk of developing a very narrow or biased perspective on the issue.

Once you've gained a broader understanding of a topic then you need to explore it. It is through such exploration that you will subsequently be able to critically appraise the topic (see chapter 10).

There are some specific techniques to help you explore topics from different angles and these can be a fruitful way to kick-start the critical thinking process! The techniques outlined here are:

1. Six Thinking Hats
2. Visual representations
3. SWOT
4. Adopting persona
5. Metaphor
6. Brainstorming
7. Consequences.

Six Thinking Hats

DeBono (1986) developed this approach, which can be used in groups or alone, in order to help people explore a topic from different perspectives.

Imagine you have six different coloured hats – white, black, yellow, green, blue and red. Each hat represents a different attitudinal predisposition, or a different way of looking at the topic, and each of the coloured hats is worn in turn.

This is what the hats stand for:

- **White hat**: The white hat is neutral. Here you examine the facts, data and the trends, without emotion. How can they be explained?
- **Black hat**: This is the pessimistic hat. Here you try your best to find problems, disadvantages and difficulties.
- **Yellow hat**: The yellow hat stands for optimism, benefits and pluses. When wearing the yellow hat you delight in identifying the benefits associated with the topic.
- **Green hat**: The green hat looks for different, fresh new ways of approaching the topic. How else might it be explored? What hasn't yet been considered?
- **Red hat**: This is the emotional hat. How do you feel about the topic? What is your intuition telling you? The red hat captures instant reactions, hunches and emotions.
- **Blue hat**: This is the summary hat. The blue hat is the 'chairperson' who pulls all the points of view together and evaluates and prioritises them.

Consciously wearing the different hats in turn can help you avoid unbalanced thinking, and ensure that you do try to view your iceberg from all angles.

TOP TIP

The Six Hats technique is also useful in group-work as it helps to ensure that different points of view are represented, something that is particularly useful in groups where there is one forceful point of view. It can also help to prevent personality clashes since different points of view are raised under the 'hat' rather than attributed personally.

Visual representations

We've mentioned this technique before in chapter 8.

Summarise your knowledge of a topic as a mindmap or flow diagram. Seeing a summary of the 'whole picture' will help you identify 'loose connections', any gaps that need filling or general trouble spots. Think of this as building your own personal Iceberg!

Drawing out what you know in this way also helps to ensure that you won't forget any component when systematically applying the critical thinking questions in chapter 10.

SWOT

SWOT is another well-known technique, which you may have used before. The aim is to generate a range of ideas about a topic using the four headings Strengths, Weaknesses, Opportunities and Threats. You generate the ideas by asking: 'What are the strengths (weaknesses, opportunities or threats) that accompany this topic or debate?'

There are only two rules:

1. Every idea you have is written down and nothing is censored.
2. You only begin to evaluate the ideas when no more can be generated.

As with Six Hats, this is a technique you can use by yourself or with others. When used in a group you are more likely to generate richer or more diverse ideas.

LOOKING AHEAD

SWOT, along with PEST, is also a popular business tool. PEST, or STEP as it is also known, follows the same principles as SWOT, but ideas are generated by asking 'What are the political, economic, social and technological factors that accompany this topic or debate?' It is possible for the ideas generated in a PEST and a SWOT to overlap.

Adopting different persona

This activity is similar to Six Thinking Hats, although here you place yourself in *specific* roles. For example, when studying the topic of Social Policy and Healthcare you might systematically place yourself in the roles of Nye Bevan, CEO of a private healthcare company, a pensioner on state benefit and leader of the two main political parties. What would each of these have to say about public policy around healthcare? And how would they justify their viewpoints?

Once again this is a technique that can be used individually or in groups. It can be used as a debating tool, in which group members debate according to the role they have adopted.

Metaphor

Lakoff and Johnson (1980) stated that:

'Most people think they can get along perfectly well without metaphor. We have found, on the contrary, that metaphor is pervasive in everyday life, not just in language but in thought and action. Our ordinary conceptual system, in terms of which we both think and act, is fundamentally metaphorical in nature.'

(p. 3)

They stated that people learn through making comparisons, and it is the resulting metaphors that drive subsequent thoughts and behaviours. The metaphors we use can help us to clarify topics, gain greater understandings, generate new ideas and resolve problems (Fernandez-Duque & Johnson 1999, Alty et al. 2000).

Metaphors can also restrict our learning. Chew and Laubichler (2003) argue that while the simplicity of many scientific metaphors is what gives them intuitive appeal, they can also lead to troubling misunderstandings. Similarly metaphor can affect our 'world view'. Lakoff (1991), for example, analysed the language used to support the proposed Gulf War. When oil is described as a 'lifeline', he argues, wealth then becomes synonymous with health, and we all want to be healthy?

You may have noticed other references to consciously using and being aware of metaphor in this book (see chapter 3 and chapter 9).

TRY THIS

What metaphors are used in your own subject? How do they direct your thinking? Can you introduce a new metaphor? How well does it work?

Can you introduce a 'forced' metaphor? Try asking yourself, for example, How is X like . . . a hair dressing salon . . . a zoo . . . or a jungle? How well does the metaphor work?

Brainstorming

This is the 'traditional' and still widely used way of exploring a topic. It's attributed to Alex Osborn in the 1960s although there are many variants on his original model. Brainstorming was originally a group attempt to find solutions to problems by allowing everyone to express ideas their spontaneously.

Individuals can also use it to explore topics in a more general way – for example everything you know, feel and believe about a topic. Like SWOT, the aim of brainstorming is to generate as many ideas as possible, without evaluation or censorship.

Ideas are only evaluated once no more can be generated and, as with SWOT, ideas need not be owned or endorsed by the person who suggests them. Variations on simple brainstorming are also possible (Richard 2003, McFadzean 1998).

DANGER!

Brainstorming has been criticised for:

- not allowing sufficient time for idea generation
- moving on to evaluation too quickly
- not evaluating!

Because brainstorming is so widely used it is often in danger of being used too casually, As with any tool, it is only as good as the person using it. Allow ample time to brainstorm and stick to the rules!

TOP TIP

Try brainstorming on post-it notes. When you come to review your ideas you can physically move them round and arrange them under different themes.

Consequences

In this technique you write out everything you know about the issue in separate statements. Then for each statement pose the question. . . . 'And the consequence is?' You continue posing this question until you can go no further. Let's look at how this technique might work if we wanted to explore Freud's belief in unconscious motivations.

Q.   *What is the consequence of this?*
A.   The theory is difficult to test empirically.

Q.   *What is the consequence of being difficult to test?*
A.   It will have less appeal to experimental psychologists.

Q.   *What is the consequence of having less appeal to experimental psychologists?*
A.   Since the dominant paradigm is experimental psychology, then psychoanalysis may not be well respected among other psychologists.

Q.   *What is the consequence of not being respected?*
A.   Freudian psychologists might become marginalised within psychology.

Q.   *What is the consequence of being marginalised?*
A.   Psychoanalysis may be ignored or overlooked by the psychological establishment, etc.

The aim is to progress your thinking to a stage that you might not normally reach through continual probing.

What next?

If you are using any of the above techniques by yourself we recommend that you try to have fun with them and enjoy them – particularly those that allow you to exercise your imagination! By allowing yourself to play with ideas in a non-threatening, 'lets see where this takes me' sort of way, you can make your own meanings and engage with the subject in a new way.

And don't worry if you find yourself sitting and daydreaming for a while – you will be in good company. Einstein also claimed that 'Imagination is more important than knowledge' and the story goes that the theory of relativity developed from a time when he sat in the sun and 'daydreamed' about taking a ride on a sunbeam!

Feeling positive has itself been associated with improved performance in problem-solving. So all the more reason to relax and enjoy? (Isen et al. 1987).

The techniques in this chapter should help you to explore and get to grips with new concepts and ideas. They should make you better equipped to undertake the more systematic and rigorous critical analysis that is described in the next chapter.

IT WORKED FOR ME

 'Probably one that you've heard before, but it works. Try carrying a "thought notebook" around with you and jotting down ideas or insights as soon as they occur to you. I used to promptly forget my flashes of inspiration but now I write them down straight away and can return to them later.'

SUMMARY

The mindmap opposite, figure 9.2, summarises the ideas in this chapter.

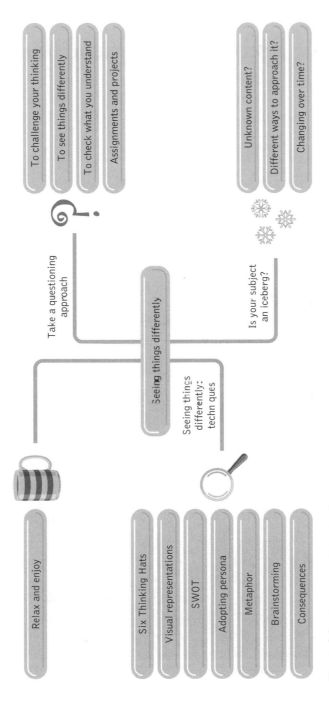

To challenge your thinking

To see things differently

To check what you understand

Assignments and projects

Unknown content?

Different ways to approach it?

Changing over time?

Take a questioning approach

Seeing things differently

Is your subject an iceberg?

Seeing things differently: techniques

Relax and enjoy

Six Thinking Hats

Visual representations

SWOT

Adopting persona

Metaphor

Brainstorming

Consequences

Figure 9.2 Summary of chapter 9

10 Becoming a critical thinker

KEY POINTS

☐ Critical thinking is an essential 'real life' skill and 'higher level' educational skill

☐ There are standardised tests available for measuring critical thinking skills

☐ You can develop your critical thinking skills

☐ The Triple A model is a working definition of critical thinking: Acquaint, Analyse and Advance

☐ The LEOR model, Logic, Emotion, Omission and Research, is useful for analysing information

☐ There may be factors that can impede or facilitate critical thinking

INTRODUCTION

Why is education so important? What is its purpose? Are you trying to perfect your memory skills? Or master the 'perfect' exam technique? Or work successfully with others? Or learn to think?

Many would claim that transferable skills such as 'working with others' and 'learning to think' are the greatest benefits of higher education. It's not unusual to hear successful adults claim they have forgotten the subject matter they studied at university and, although some job roles require specific subject knowledge, many do not. In these cases graduate trainees, often with different academic backgrounds, typically acquire company-relevant knowledge through a combination of formal learning and practical experience. Such recruits are valued for their generic skills such as problem-solving and critical thinking rather than degree discipline alone.

In this chapter we're going to explore the topic of critical thinking through four questions:

1. What is 'critical thinking'?
2. Am I a critical thinker?
3. How can I improve my critical thinking?
4. Are there any barriers to critical thinking?

By the end of the chapter, you should be able to use your critical thinking skills to refine your own opinion on the purpose and value of education.

1. WHAT IS CRITICAL THINKING?

Have you ever watched a comedy show in which one actor talks increasingly loudly, in the hope that the foreign listener will eventually understand what is being said? It's funny only because we all know that raising the volume does not improve comprehension!

Yet, in our experience something similar often happens in education. Does any of the following feedback sound familiar?

'Good work, although very descriptive – you needed to include more critical appraisal.'
'A sound summary, but lacking thorough critical evaluation.'
'Good as far as it goes – the next step is to increase the amount of critical comment.'

If you're ever received similar feedback how did you feel? We'd guess that the most common reactions include:

'But I thought I had been critical. . . .'
'I don't understand what I'm meant to do.'
'I worked so hard on that essay – it must
have deserved a better grade.'

Just as talking more loudly cannot increase language comprehension so repeated requests for more critical reasoning cannot ensure it happens. In both instances there is a skill to be learnt.

TRY THIS

In order to identify the skills required, let's think about the meaning of the phrase 'critical thinking'. Take a look at some of the definitions of critical thinking presented here and try to identify the key ideas contained in each.

Critical thinking is. . . .

Reasonable and reflective thinking that is focused upon deciding what to believe or do.

(*Norris & Ennis 1989*)

The art of thinking about thinking while thinking to make thinking better.

(*Paul & Heaslip 1995*)

Thinking that is purposeful, reasoned and goal directed – the kind of thinking involved in solving problems, formulating inferences, calculating likelihoods and making decisions when the thinker is using skills that are thoughtful and effective for the particular context and type of thinking task.

(*Halpern 1995*)

An investigation whose purpose is to explore a situation, phenomenon, question or problem to arrive at a hypothesis or conclusion about it, that integrates all available information and that can therefore be convincingly justified.

(*Kurfiss 2000*)

An awareness of a set of interrelated critical questions, plus the ability and willingness to ask and answer them at appropriate times.

(*Browne & Keeley 2004*)

There are numerous definitions of 'critical thinking', but what do they have in common? Drawing on your own experience, and the key ideas identified above, have a go at writing your own definition of critical thinking.

How did you do? Your definition should aim to show *what* critical thinking involves and perhaps *how* it differs from other forms of thinking. If your definition included words such as 'evaluating', 'questioning' with 'conscious', 'directed' or 'focused' then you are definitely on the right lines!

Good critical thinkers don't accept facts at face value. This doesn't mean that you become distrustful or cynical, instead it means that you should carefully consider the validity of every idea, concept or statement that you meet in your study. You do not have to agree with all the ideas or theories that you encounter, but any criticism must be based on sound thinking rather than an emotional reaction or 'gut' feelings.

Critical thinking is like buying a secondhand car!

There are probably many occasions when you already exhibit critical thinking. Shopping for a major purchase is a time when most of us become skilled critical thinkers. Imagine that you want to buy a secondhand car within a fixed budget. You visit a car salesman, who says he has 'the perfect car for you' and you agree to look at the vehicle. Which of the following best captures how you will behave?

1.   You hand over the cash on first sight.
2.   You try to decide if this is indeed the perfect car for you.

There may be times when you 'fall in love' with a particular car at first sight and allow your emotions to override more rational thoughts. We suspect that, most of the time, most of us would want to take the second option. Part of this decision would involve thinking carefully about the information given by the salesman.

TRY THIS

Firstly, complete the 'thought bubbles' below in response to what the salesman is saying:

'This is the ideal car for you.'

'It's been exceptionally well looked after. Only one careful owner since new and it has been serviced regularly.'

'Not only is this car a great little goer, but it's just been fitted with new tyres and a new clutch.'

'It does 35 mpg and this model is renowned for its reliability. I'd strongly recommend that you give it a test drive – it's bound to sell quickly!'

See page 262 for our ideas. Now read through what you've written and tick the table below to show whether these terms are evident in one or more of your own thought bubbles.

	Applies	**Does not apply**
Questioning		
Evaluating		
Deciding		
Intentional		
Objective		
Non-emotional		
Rational		
Evidence-based		
Logical		

Although we may associate 'critical thinking' with education, the exercise above should demonstrate that you employ critical thinking in many other contexts. Your role as a critical learner is to approach all ideas in the same way that you would the secondhand car salesman.

Critical thinking in education

In each of your assignments and every course learning outcome, there should be a key verb intended to show you how to engage with the material. Commonly used verbs include compare, contrast, summarise, consider, describe and state.

Such verbs are not chosen randomly. They are selected after taking the level or stage of the course, and the specific aims of an assignment or learning outcome, into consideration.

One of the challenges that you face as a learner is to recognise the types of thinking skills that these different verbs require you to demonstrate.

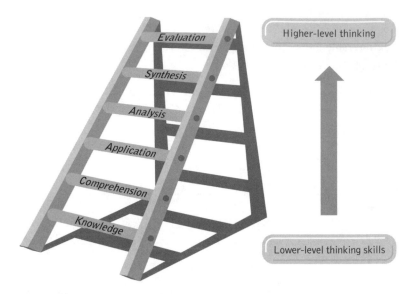

Figure 10.1 Bloom's hierarchy of cognitive skills

Educationalist Benjamin Bloom (1956) proposed a hierarchy of thinking skills which is still used in education today (see figure 10.1).

This 'thinking skills' ladder runs from 'concrete' thinking (such as knowing facts) through to 'abstract' thinking. The abstract skill of evaluation, or critical thinking, sits at the top of the ladder.

TRY THIS

Educationalists associate different verbs with the different rungs of the ladder. Imagine that you want a group of students to complete several assignments, each focusing on one of the levels above. What verbs could you use to guide student thinking styles at each stage of the hierarchy?

Table 10.1 illustrates some of the verbs that are frequently employed at each level of the hierarchy. So, when learners are expected to evaluate they might be asked to 'critically appraise' or 'judge' as well as 'evaluate'.

In reality there is often some overlap between the verbs associated with the different rungs of the hierarchy; the important point is that there is an

Table 10.1   Verbs used at each stage of the thinking skills hierarchy

Knowledge	Comprehension	Application	Analysis	Synthesis	Evaluation
Label	Describe	Demonstrate	Compare	Organise	Judge
Memorise	Explain	Illustrate	Contrast	Create	Appraise
List	Report	Apply	Distinguish	Combine	Assess
Order	Re-write	Solve	Relate	Review	Justify

accepted cognitive continuum from 'rote learning' through to 'what's good about this'? In order to reach the top rung of the ladder you must have climbed the lower rungs first, since you can't evaluate without first having factual knowledge and understanding.

Look again at some of your recent assignment titles or course learning outcomes, with the following questions in mind:

- What cognitive instruction terms are included?
- Can you spot any 'progression' of terms, perhaps from one year to another or from the start to the end of the course?
- If you are registered on a postgraduate programme do you notice any change from your undergraduate days?

TRY THIS

We believe that all courses, regardless of the subject, lend themselves to the full hierarchy of thinking skills. For example:

- Medical students must memorise anatomy; yet reaching the correct diagnosis and deciding on optimal treatment for an individual patient invariably requires critical thinking.
- History students memorise dates but choosing between two conflicting historical accounts requires critical thinking.
- Sociology students must be able to describe Functionalism and Interactionism. Yet evaluating these two perspectives requires critical thinking.

Consider some of the topics that you are currently studying. What have you memorised and what has involved critical thinking?

TOP TIP

When you are asked to evaluate in an essay or exam, it is important that you reach the top of the ladder very quickly, since this will help you to achieve maximum grades. Lengthy description is usually at the expense of evaluation and it does not attract the marks reserved for good critical thinking. We've yet to hear of any essay feedback saying there was too much critical appraisal!

2. AM I A CRITICAL THINKER?

Just as you can assess your preferred intelligence, learning style or reading speed using specifically designed tests, so you can assess your critical thinking skills. There are three main tests designed for this purpose.

The Watson Glaser Critical Thinking Appraisal (WGCTA) test

- Developed by Watson and Glaser (1952).
- Based on five different but interdependent types of 'critical thinking':
  - drawing inferences
  - making assumptions
  - deductive reasoning
  - interpretation
  - argument discrimination.

The California Critical Thinking Skills Test (CCTST)

- Developed by Facione (1990) following a survey among members of the American Philosophical Association about what precisely constitutes critical thinking.
- Incorporates five cognitive skills:

- induction
- deduction
- inference
- analysis
- evaluation.

The Cornell Critical Thinking Test

- Developed by Ennis and Millman (1985).
- Includes multiple-choice questions addressing:

  - definition
  - induction
  - deduction
  - prediction
  - fallacy
  - credibility
  - assumptions identification.

Each of these tests measure critical thinking, as defined by the test developers, and each is independently produced and marketed. There is an enormous amount of background information and data available for each test; norms are available, validity has been examined and each has been widely used in research.

Educational organisations or employers sometimes use these tests to assess levels of critical thinking. Scores on the WGCTA, for example, have been shown to be predictive of success in a range of educational programmes (Gadzella et al. 1997). You might want to enquire whether your educational institution has purchased the rights to administer one of these tests.

TRY THIS

Table 10.2 suggests a few diagnostic questions to help you consider your own critical thinking. Try to answer each question using 'Hardly Ever' (HE), 'Sometimes' (S) or 'Nearly Always' (NA).

Table 10.2 Diagnostic questions

Question	HE	S	NA
1. Does your assignment feedback typically praise your critical appraisal?			
2. When you first hear a controversial argument do you consider all angles or you do you reach an 'instant' decision?			
3. Are you able to articulate and justify the views you hold?			
4. Do you easily spot weaknesses in other people's arguments?			
5. Are you reflective – do you review and analyse personal experiences and events?			
6. Are you able to present an internally consistent argument on controversial topics?			
7. Are your opinions usually underpinned by logic and not just emotion?			
8. Would your friends describe you as fair and open-minded?			
9. How often do you query the material that you are presented with in the classroom or lecture theatre?			
10. How often do you reconsider your views when you're presented with more information?			

If your answers are mainly 'nearly always' then we think that you are likely to be well on the way to being a good critical thinker, since these are some of the attributes that we associate with critical thinking and evaluation. Personal reflection and review are also an important element of critical thinking. See chapter 12 for more detail.

TOP TIP

It's usually more difficult to carry out critical appraisal effectively when you feel emotionally involved in the topic. No matter how passionate you feel about a subject or debate, try to adopt the position of a disinterested onlooker when critically appraising the arguments. Chapter 9, Generating Ideas, should help here.

The good news is that your critical thinking skills are not fixed but can be improved. In the next section we look at how to develop and improve your critical thinking abilities.

3. HOW CAN I IMPROVE MY CRITICAL THINKING?

As shown above there are many definitions of critical thinking around. We've called our working definition of critical thinking the Triple A model. The Triple A model aims to summarise the key stages of critical thinking.

TRIPLE A MODEL OF CRITICAL THINKING

1. **Acquaint** yourself with the ideas that are being presented. What key points are being made?
2. **Analyse** the arguments underpinning these ideas. Are they flawed in any way?
3. **Advance** the situation. What are the implications of this debate?

At each stage of the Triple A model there are different strategies that you can use to help improve your critical thinking skills:

Stage 1 Acquaint

The aim here is to gain an understanding of the theory or concept that you wish to evaluate.

You first need to consider where to look for relevant information, which books or journals will be useful and the best reading approach to use:

- If possible begin by looking at the information sources cited on your reading lists.
- Alternatively, look for other books or articles published by the same authors.
- Try reading simple or introductory texts before moving to 'higher level' sources.
- Make sure you have the skills you need to undertake an effective literature search.
- Allow sufficient time to locate the information you need.

Assuming the information you have is in print format, you'll probably use all three main reading skills. You will need to scan and skim when making your book or journal selection, and later engage in focused reading as you familiarise yourself with some of the nuances and subtleties. (For more advice on reading strategies see chapter 6.)

Even topics that predominantly involve visual or auditory evaluation – such as art or music – normally require some background reading in order to appreciate the historical or technical context.

Stage 2 Analyse

Once you have an understanding you then need to analyse the theory or concept. One way to do this is to ask a series of questions under the headings Logic, Emotion, Omission and Research (LEOR), as shown in figure 10.2.

Logic
Is the theory or argument consistent or does it contradict itself?
Does each conclusion follow naturally from the preceding points?
Are there any circular arguments?
Are all the claims justified or are assumptions being made?
Are all the points relevant to the overall argument?

Emotion
Is the argument overly emotional?
Does the author have a vested interest in persuading the reader?
Is the argument presented fairly or is there bias?
Does the argument lack balance or subtlety?

Omission
Does any vital information appear to be missing?
Is any information distorted or presented inaccurately?
Is any information lacking in precision?
Are there are alternative explanations or viewpoints that are not included or considered?

Research
If research data are included then you need to assess their validity and reliability. The questions that help you do this can be summarised as '5Ws and one H':

Why?	Why was the original research undertaken? • What were the original research objectives?
What?	What type of research was undertaken? • Surveys? Experiments? Qualitative research (e.g. in-depth interviews)?
Where?	Where was the research undertaken? • In which country(ies)? Urban or rural settings? • In a laboratory or in a natural setting?
When?	1. What year(s)? 2. Does the time of day, day of the week, or time of the year matter?

Who?	1. Who took part in the research?
	      • What type of person participated in the research? What criteria were used to allow entry into the research, e.g. age, gender, social class?
	      • How many? How were they found?
	      • Does the sample represent the total population of interest?
	 2. Who commissioned the research?
	      • e.g. government/charity/pressure group/company
	 3. Who published the research? Was the report peer-reviewed?

How?	1. How were the data collected? e.g.
	      • attitudinal data?
	      • observational data?
	      • self-reported behavioural data?
	      • knowledge data?
	 2. How are the data reported?
	      • Does the reporting show any bias?
	      • Have the appropriate statistical tests been used?
	      • Is the use of percentages fair or misleading?
	      • Are graphs a fair representation of the data, or do they 'distort' the data in any way?

Figure 10.2 The LEOR questions

If you feel that you want to include additional questions under each heading don't worry. The headings are there to help you remember the *types* of questions you should ask, and the questions we've included are not intended to be dogmatic or exhaustive.

THINGS TO THINK ABOUT

When thinking critically try asking these two questions:

1. Is this a theoretical argument and am I convinced by the quality of the argument expressed?
2. Is research data included and have I assessed the quality of that data?

TRY THIS

Take a moment to read through the paragraph below, which presents a fictional argument about smoking in the UK:

There are currently around 12 million adult smokers in Great Britain and prevalence is highest in the 20–24-year age group. Smokers are more likely to come from lower socio-economic groups, and these groups also begin smoking at a younger age. As with so much else, it appears to be the middle classes who are receiving the lion share of smoking cessation and healthcare initiatives. Meanwhile, the number of teenage pregnancies and sexually transmitted diseases continues to rise in the UK, and once again these affect the lower socio-economic classes more than others. The continued representation in the media of smoking as an 'adult' behaviour and one which enhances sexual attractiveness is negatively influencing these vulnerable young people, who find themselves in a cycle of smoking, drinking and casual sex. If we want to reduce the number of new smokers we must target these at-risk groups with literature on smoking and lung cancer, and show the pain and stress that this disease brings to both the sufferers and their familes. It is also time to conscientiously sue those vendors, who are presently escaping prosecution, who sell tobacco to under-age consumers.

What were your initial thoughts as you read through the paragraph above? What did you think of the arguments presented?

Let's look at this same paragraph now, using the four headings, **LEOR:**

Logic

- It is not consistent to claim that, because more smokers come from lower socio-economic classes, these groups are receiving less health-promotion resource. They might receive the same amount or even more resource, but respond to it differently. Different messages around smoking cessation might, for example, have a differential impact on different socio-economic groups.
- This new topic of sexually transmitted disease rates is not made relevant to the overall discussion on smoking.
- The first implicit assumption is that smokers are at greater risk of the STD or pregnancy than non-smokers. Yet nothing is presented to substantiate that claim.
- A second assumption is that tobacco advertising has resulted in increased sexual activity among the young. Once again, there is nothing to support this argument.
- Although the assertion that more smoking-cessation campaigns delivered to lower socio-economic groups might be considered reasonable, there is nothing to support the view that 'disease' campaigns should be used. Although a 'disease' campaign is advocated we don't know if this is the most effective campaign material to use. Would 'saving money' or 'bad breath' campaigns have more impact?
- The conclusion does not relate to the earlier information, nor is the statement that vendors are currently not prosecuted justified. In order to examine the truth of this assertion we need to see some data.

Is the argument consistent or does it contradict itself?

Does each conclusion follow naturally from the preceding points?

Are there any circular arguments?

Are all the claims justified or are assumptions being made?

Are all the points relevant to the overall argument?

Emotion

- Some emotional terms are included in the paragraph. The phrase 'lion share' implies a large difference in resource allocation, but this assertion is not justified in any way.
- Since the author of the paragraph is not shown we do not know if the writer has a vested interest. Who do you think is more likely to have written the article – the tobacco industry, a government department or an anti-smoking pressure group?

Is the argument overly emotional?

Does the author have a vested interest in persuading the reader?

Is the argument presented fairly or is it biased?

Omission

- The figures included are not contextualised and so important information is not included. Does the figure of 12 million smokers represent an increase or decrease of the number of smokers over time?
- Is the amount of tobacco smoked increasing or decreasing over time?
- What is the actual prevalence of smokers across different social groups?
- What is the evidence around sales to under-age smokers and rates of prosecution?
- What is the evidence to suggest that 'disease' campaigns prevent the uptake of smoking any more than, say, campaigns that focus on saving money or 'here and now' health-related issues such as bad breath?
- Although some information is provided it is not enough to see the whole picture and so the argument is not fairly presented.
- The author's identity is not disclosed. Does this matter? Why?

Is any vital information missing?

Is any information distorted or presented inaccurately?

Is any information lacking in precision?

Are there alternative explanations or viewpoints that are not included or considered?

Research

Although some figures on smoking are included they are not referenced and there are outstanding questions. Specifically:

5Ws and 1 H

- Who undertook the research into smoking prevalence?
- Who participated in the research?
- How were the data collected?
- When were the data collected – are these recent or historical figures?

Did you find that helpful? Some of the points mentioned here may have jumped out when you first read the paragraph on smoking. Yet, when faced with a complex or sophisticated argument, it can be difficult to exercise good critical judgement. The LEOR questions should help you remain focused.

TOP TIP

Don't be surprised if you are asked to critically appraise complex areas where there are no clear solutions. Even 'experts' may not agree in their critical analysis of a situation – property market predictions, explanations of improvements in 'A' level results over time and the safety of the MMR vaccine are just three examples which demonstrate diversity among expert analysis. Your job is to decide which viewpoint you support and why.

Logical fallacies

There are also a number of different ways of arguing illogically that you can look out for in your studies. They are known as logical fallacies and here are examples of three common fallacies:

- **Fallacy of false alternatives**: Only two alternatives are put forward and a conclusion is reached. Yet there are other alternatives that have not been considered. For example, the cause of climate change is either de-forestation or increased levels of carbon dioxide emissions through rising car use. . . .

- **Fallacy of false cause**: An earlier event is said to have caused a later event even though no evidence of causality is presented. Louise's Granny used to believe that the bad weather she experienced shortly after the first lunar landing was the direct result of space travel . . .

- **Fallacy of ignorance**: Something is presented as the truth simply because there is no opposing evidence. No one has shown that genetically modified food damages your health, therefore it is safe . . .

Many logical fallacies have been identified. If you want to explore this further then two current internet sites are included in the list at the end of the book, although you may prefer to conduct your own search.

The LEOR activity above involved only a small amount of research data. The next activity will provide you with more practice with the 'R' of 'LEOR':

TRY THIS

Read through the fictional account below, and then apply the LEOR questions.

New research shows that concern about the lack of student accommodation is one reason why students do not apply to university. A recent survey among University of Can-Do students showed that 69 per cent of respondents cited accommodation availability as a factor they had taken into consideration before applying to the university. 81 per cent stated that the provision of accommodation for first-year students was 'very poor' and 42 per cent rated their current accommodation as 'very poor' in size, cost and facilities.

It appears that the accommodation shortage can only worsen. In 1995 100 per cent of first-year students were given university accommodation but by 2005 this figure had fallen to 77 per cent. Drop-outs during this time have risen from 12 per cent to almost 20 per cent of students, which highlights the effect that accommodation shortages have upon student commitment.

Because this argument is based almost entirely on research data, the **R** questions become more pertinent. Did you include any of the points below in your answers?

Logic

The explanation of university drop-out is not logically complete – there may be other reasons to account for this.

Is the argument consistent or does it contradict itself

Emotion

We do not know who authored the paragraph – is there a vested interest?

Is the argument presented fairly or is it biased?

Omission

- We don't know what percentage of students received university accommodation between 1995 and 2005.

Is any vital information missing?

Research

- The original research objectives are not given and the aims are not made explicit.
- The research is described as a survey.
- Was research undertaken at other universities as the University of Can-do may not be representative of all universities. Can you think of any ways in which older non-campus universities, for example, may face very different housing issues than newer campus universities? Or universities with higher proportions of overseas students? You might also want to consider where the research is published since not all journals review articles prior to publication.

5 Ws and 1 H
Why?
What?
Where?

- Does it matter when the survey was undertaken?   When?
  Would you expect any differences if students were
  surveyed in the first week of an academic year or
  the last week?

- We are not told who participated nor the type   Who?
  of student that took part. Would it matter if
  they were all from one type of university faculty or
  from the same undergraduate year? Do you think
  that first-year undergraduates face the same
  housing issues as second- or third-year students?

- We also know very little about who took part. Would
  you expect different responses if only students visiting
  the student accommodation office were recruited?

- How were the data collected? We are not told how   How?
  the questionnaires were administered nor the exact
  questions included. Question wording can influence
  answers. For example, the question 'Don't you agree
  that universities do not do very much to help students
  find suitable accommodation?' is more leading than
  one that asks 'How helpful are universities in helping
  students to find accommodation?'

- How well are data reported? There are two or three
  concerns that you might have identified. Firstly the
  data is reported as percentages, yet we do not know
  how many students took part in research.
  Presenting percentages without including the overall
  number of respondents is not very helpful. If only
  20 students participated overall, then even high
  percentages would still refer to very low absolute
  numbers of students.

- Figures are presented for 1995 and 2005 but there
  is no interim data. If student numbers had fallen
  gradually over this period then you might feel more
  convinced that there is a trend that will continue.
  Alternatively, was there a sharp decrease in one
  year only? A change in educational policy, for
  example, might result in a sudden decrease in the
  number of undergraduate students.

We hope that this account shows how the 'five Ws and an H' can help you to assess the strengths and weakness of a research study and the potency of its' conclusions or recommendations.

IT WORKED FOR ME

'My advice to new learners is to be brave and always try to adopt a position or an argument. Thanks mainly to a really supportive teacher I've realised that I learn far more by evaluating and taking a position than I do through describing. Sometimes I miss something very obvious, or my thinking is illogical, yet my grade has still been respectable – it's as though my lecturers would prefer to see some attempt at critical thinking, even if it is flawed, than none at all. So, think positively, have faith in yourself and have a go at developing your own arguments!'

TOP TIP

It is likely that much of what you read will be a mix of both logic- and research-based argument. Try to remember:

*   Factual claims often require supporting evidence to be convincing (try asking if you are reading an opinion masquerading as a fact).
*   Data does not speak for itself but always requires interpretation.

Stage 3 Advance

And finally, the third stage of the Triple A model which is *advance*. Take a look at the following paragraph about personal autonomy.

Do we have the freedom to choose the person we want to be? Does our biology determine who we are? Does our environment determine who we are? This has been one of the great debates in psychology and philosophy for hundreds of years. The extreme biological model argues that our genes determine who we are. The extreme social model argues that the culture we are born into makes us who we are. Alternative models propose that through conscious thought we have the capacity to examine ourselves and bring about change.

One way to advance your critical thinking is by taking a step back and asking some 'big picture' questions. Instead of focusing purely on the detail of the theory try asking 'Why is this an important question?', 'What are the implications and applications of the arguments presented?' and 'Is there a completely different way of addressing the question?'

What happens when you apply 'big picture' questions to the example of personal autonomy above? Although the paragraph is short this debate has HUGE implications. Does acceptance of biological determinism remove personal responsibility for our own actions? For example, if a 'criminal gene' was identified are criminals 'born' and not 'made'? What would be the implications for our current legal system? Should we continue to invest in rehabilitation programmes? Or should there be greater investment into gene research? What would be the role of psychologists or probation officers?

Being able to evaluate a debate in this manner is another way of demonstrating your critical thinking skills. The big questions add an extra dimension to the debate so try to get into the habit of asking yourself 'Why is this topic important?'

IT WORKED FOR ME

'One thing I've learned as an undergraduate, is that critical thinking takes time. If I write an essay the night before the due submission date, then either it is descriptive or the thinking is flawed. So now, I try to give myself plenty of thinking time beforehand. It doesn't need to be a huge block of time; in fact I've found small pockets of time more useful. It doesn't have to be "formal" study time either. I sometimes try and explore academic ideas when I'm engaged in fairly "mindless" activities, for example when I'm working as a shelf stacker at weekends or when I'm in the bath.'

4. ARE THERE ANY BARRIERS TO CRITICAL THINKING?

We've said that critical thinking is a highly valued skill. Can you think of any possible barriers to being a critical thinker? We asked a student called Andrew to consider this and here is an extract from our subsequent conversation:

Louise: Did you identify some potential barriers to critical thinking?

Andrew: I've never considered this before so I've tried to guess what might act as a barrier, or what might make a difference. My first thought was that family background might be important. Some families encourage children to put forward their points of view far more than others, so perhaps that impacts on how much critical thinking they later display?

Louise: That's a great suggestion. We're not aware of any research looking purely at 'parental encouragement' alone but some research has investigated differences relating to social class. A study of over 500 Hong Kong university students showed higher social class students demonstrated superior critical thinking skills as well as a more positive predisposition towards critical thinking (Cheung et al. 2001). And many studies have highlighted class differences in overall educational attainment and motivation (Felner et al. 1995, Argyle 1994). As with much else, it seems plausible that earlier experiences may impact later behaviours in this area.

Andrew: I also wondered if cultural background matters? I've heard that there are often differences in educational practices between countries, so I wondered if there are cultures where critical appraisal is not encouraged? In a highly censored society for example? Or some countries might want to actively discourage students questioning the status quo for political reasons?

Louise: Again, that's a really good point. Although we can't claim that political sensitivity lies behind differences in educational systems, some research suggests differences in approach to critical thinking between cultures (Yeh & Chen 2003, Howe 2004). One study, for example, found that Australian students had a more positive predisposition to critical thinking than Hong Kong Chinese students (Tiwari et al. 2003).

So, both personal experiences and societal influences *may* affect critical thinking skills. Did you have anything else on your list?

Andrew: I got stuck after that – there didn't seem to be any more obvious barriers! I wondered if there are individual barriers. For example, are there any personality types that make better critical thinkers than others, for example?

Louise: Well there are certainly some essential personal attributes and practices that go hand-in-hand with critical thinking. One of these is metacognition a term coined by Flavell (1976). Metacognition is the ability to stand back and consciously think about your thinking processes. It involves reflecting on what you currently know, identifying gaps and needs, and monitoring and directing your own thought processes. By thinking about your own thinking you can plan and direct future thinking and learning strategies. Metacogniton is a hugely valuable life skill! Outside formal learning situations you may receive little regular feedback and so it becomes even more important that you can appraise your own thinking processes.

And finally, one other potential barrier that we haven't considered yet is the way in which education is organised. In a recent review of the literature, Pithers and Soden (2000) identified certain types of teacher behaviour, a curriculum focused on subject matter rather than debate, or a culture of oppression as each being a barrier to critical thinking.

Andrew: So what sorts of positive educational influences are there?

Louise: There is some evidence that students prefer certain teaching styles above others, for example Problem Based Learning, and that these preferred styles are associated with improved critical thinking skills (Streinert 2004, Hay & Vincent 2004). And the current consensus seems to be that critical thinking should be at the centre of subject teaching and not taught solely as an independent subject in isolation from others (Pithers 2000, Maudsley & Strivens

2000). Even when you have only limited direct influence over your programme delivery, you can still consciously reflect on your thinking processes and bring critical thinking to every subject that you study.

Andrew: OK, great. I'll try doing that and see what happens to my grades!

LOOKING AHEAD

This chapter has focused on becoming a 'critical thinker'. Yet engaging in critical thinking and applying the results of that thinking are not the same (Seymour et al. 2003). Greenwood et al. (2000), for example, found that nurses did not always implement the conclusion they had arrived at through critical analysis. The nurses' explanations for this included the 'people they were working with' and 'hospital policy'. Other possible reasons why people do not apply the results of their critical thinking might include:

- manager or peer pressure
- lack of any reward
- lack of experience in managing change
- an organisational culture that favours the 'status quo'
- suggesting change often makes people unpopular.

Why not look ahead and consider whether there are any personal skills that will help you to implement the results of your critical appraisal either now or in the future?

IT WORKED FOR ME

'A small group of us meet regularly to bounce ideas around and challenge each other. It's been so successful it's almost a social event now! Two weeks before each assignment is due we meet up to discuss the topic and each bring along a snack to share. My critical thinking skills have really developed through this exploration and debate. Despite this group discussion, we still each produce an individual essay – yet one that each of us feels is richer because of the wider discussions.'

SUMMARY

Let's quickly summarise the Triple A model before showing a chapter overview (figure 10.3).

- Step 1 **Acquaint**
- Step 2 **Analyse**: Use **LEOR** to help you, as appropriate
- Step 3 **Advance**

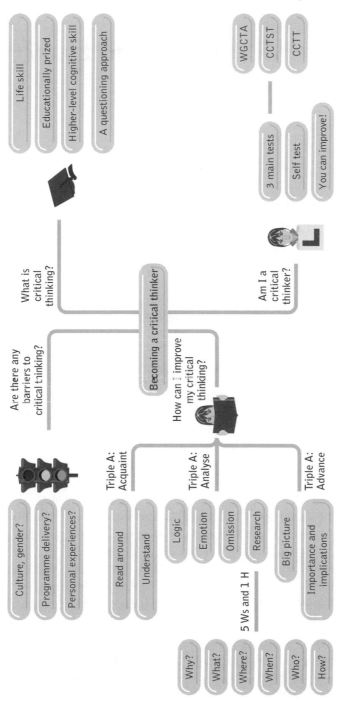

Figure 10.3 Summary of chapter 10

11 How to Write an Essay

'Good writing is bad writing that was rewritten.'
Railbert (1996)

KEY POINTS

☐ Essay-writing draws on reading, note-taking, and critical thinking

☐ Developing expertise in writing requires time and practice

☐ You should consider purpose, preparation, process, structure, style and content when essay writing

☐ The ability to communicate clearly in writing is a valuable skill

INTRODUCTION

Most, if not all, formal study requires some writing, although the nature of the writing will vary. This chapter focuses on essay-writing, the traditional method of assessing student learning, and we explore the craft of essay writing by examining these seven areas:

1. **Purpose:** What is my objective here? (page 211)
2. **Preparation:** What should I do first? (page 212)
3. **Process:** Is there a recommended approach to writing? (page 216)
4. **Structure:** What form should my essay take? (page 221)
5. **Style:** What kind of writing do I use? (page 222)
6. **Content:** What subject matter do I include? (page 228)
7. **Review:** What can I learn for the future? (page 231)

1. PURPOSE: WHAT IS MY OBJECTIVE HERE?

Before you begin any writing assignment, you should be able to answer the following questions:

- What do I want to say?
- Who is my audience?
- Why are they reading what I've written?

Although these questions may appear straightforward, many people find them tricky to answer when applied to course essays. How would you respond? The answers to these questions will influence how you write.

Many academics feel driven to write because of a passionate belief in their subject, yet as a learner you may often be uncertain of what you want to say. It is much easier to write when you have a clear idea of your intended message and the preparation stage can help you identify this.

Your 'official' audience is the person who marks the essay. However, we recommend that you also write with an artificial audience in mind, such as an intelligent, educated 'lay person' with an interest in the subject. Your lecturer will read your essay in order to assess your learning, while your fictitious audience will read to be informed. Your essay will be much stronger if you take account of both audiences.

It can be intimidating to write with your lecturer, an acknowledged expert, in mind. Norton et al. (2001)'s research on essay-writing uncovered a number of misguided beliefs that students followed in the hope of pleasing the assessor and improving their grades.

These included:

- not criticising the lecturer's views
- using jargon/big words/technical terms to try and impress the lecturer
- trying to include obscure information, or information not covered in the lectures, to try and make a better impression
- putting more effort into the first essay to try and create a positive first impression
- writing over the word limit.

Such behaviours are not recommended and instead of helping may actually hinder your grade.

2. PREPARATION: WHAT SHOULD I DO FIRST?

Before you can begin to write an essay you need to be clear about your task. This requires good preparation.

TRY THIS

Rate the statements below to review how you usually prepare for essay writing

	Never	Occasionally	Sometimes	Usually	Always
a) I allow enough time to research my essays	☐	☐	☐	☐	☐
b) I allow enough time to write my essays	☐	☐	☐	☐	☐
c) I take care to interpret and understand the essay title	☐	☐	☐	☐	☐
d) I read all the student advice and marking criteria	☐	☐	☐	☐	☐
e) I think about what I already know, and identify knowledge gaps and ways to fill them	☐	☐	☐	☐	☐
f) I keep a record of all my reading	☐	☐	☐	☐	☐
g) I develop a position on the topic before I begin writing	☐	☐	☐	☐	☐
h) If I am unsure of what is expected, I ask my tutor	☐	☐	☐	☐	☐

Which answers did you select? We hope you had a clean sweep of 'always', but if not, let's take a closer look at each point.

a) I allow enough time to research my essays

Try working backwards from the due submission date to allocate the time you need. Allow time for:

- searching the literature
- reading and critically appraising the literature
- inter-library requests
- recalling on-loan texts
- other studies
- other areas of your life e.g. birthdays, work, public holidays, vacations and family time.

b) I allow enough time to write my essays

Essay-writing falls under the category of 'Things in Life that *Always* Take Much Longer than Anticipated' so allow even more time than you might expect. Even smaller tasks such as proofreading, or compiling the reference list, can be surprisingly time-consuming. If you have to deal with any unexpected events e.g. illness, then keep a record of dates in case you need to request an extension or ask for 'exceptional circumstances' to be taken into consideration. A late submission without permission may not be accepted or may carry an automatic penalty.

c) I take care to interpret and understand the title

It can be tempting to read a title and start working immediately, only to realise later that your initial interpretation was wrong. Consider the title carefully, until you are confident you understand what is required. Are you clear about:

- exactly what the question is asking?
- how many parts there are to the question?
- which parts, if any, are the most important?

- any hidden subtleties in the question?
- the degree of flexibility you have to select a particular approach? (see the Q&A section on page 229).

DANGER!

It is absolutely fine, and even helpful, to discuss the title with your peers. Any collaboration after this point may leave you open to accusations of cheating or plagiarism. You should *write* your essay alone and not in a group.

d) I read all the student advice and marking criteria

You need to do this at the preparation stage and not leave it until the point of submission!

Some courses/institutions have very explicit competencies and marking criteria for assignments and marks are automatically deducted if work does not strictly adhere to the given criteria. Other institutions may have more subjective or flexible marking schemes. We recommend you find out as much as you can about exactly how your work will be graded. In many cases you'll be given specific advice, which may even include guidance on the preferred 'house style' and whether there are penalties for exceeding the word limit.

TRY THIS

Have a go at grading essays by swapping clean copies of previously marked essays with other course members. If marking criteria were provided then use those, otherwise you can apply/adapt our generic marking grid on page 263.

As you read the essay put yourself into the assessor role and consider the following:

- What grade will you award overall?
- How will you justify that grade?
- How will you phrase your feedback so that it is balanced, truthful and motivating?

You may want to read through the section on peer assessment (page 102, chapter 5) before undertaking this activity, since it requires high levels of trust and good interpersonal skills.

e) I think about what I already know and identify knowledge gaps and ways to fill them

Reflecting on the essay title and student advice will help you to assess your knowledge and identify any gaps. You then need to consider which resources will help you improve. Try to make this as easy as possible for yourself:

- Use your recommended reading lists, lecture notes and handouts before searching further.
- Check out the learning style tips for literature searches on pages 71–6 (chapter 4).
- Use the reading techniques in chapter 6 to help you read texts in the most appropriate way.
- Don't allow yourself to be distracted by interesting, yet irrelevant information.
- Recognise when to stop. Don't use extended literature searching and reading as an avoidance technique or displacement activity to delay the essay writing!

f) I keep a record of all my reading

Have you ever completed an essay only to discover that you do not have full details of all the references? Don't let it happen. (Refer to chapter 8 for tips on note-taking and record-keeping.)

g) I develop a position on the topic before I begin writing

An essay is a balanced argument, expressed in writing, usually in support of a particular point of view. In order to make the writing process easier you need to be clear about your own position and understand the supporting and opposing arguments. Make sure you understand the positions and arguments that are adopted in the literature, and ask yourself how convincing you find them. What are the strengths of the different theories, perspectives or accounts that you are reading? What are the weaknesses? Which aspects are central to your essay? Some of the chapters in this book should help you to develop your own point of view. (See especially chapters 8 and 9.)

h) If I am unsure of what is expected, I ask my tutor

Lecturers should not mind if you seek clarification around an essay title. Expect to be asked for your own interpretation first so that the lecturer can see that you have actively considered the assignment and can understand what is causing confusion. It is better to ask than feel anxious.

3. PROCESS: IS THERE A RECOMMENDED APPROACH TO WRITING?

There are many possible approaches to the process of writing an essay. Some students sit down and write and write, while others work in a more piece-meal fashion. Learners are often advised to 'follow the process that works best for you'. Yet often the essay-writing process is simply a 'habit' developed over time, rather than a conscious and deliberate attempt to find the best technique. Is this the case for you?

What is your reaction to the statement below?

'I have tried different approaches to essay-writing and am confident that I use the one that gives me best results.'

TRY THIS

Drawing on your own knowledge and experience what advice would you give a new learner on the 'best' essay-writing process?

Our advice is shown below.

Begin with an essay plan

Use your preparation time to formulate an essay plan. You need to include the key points, ideas and evidence that you will use to support your position and then decide on a logical order. When you begin drafting the essay you may find that you want to modify, extend or even completely rewrite the plan. Don't worry if this happens, for most people writing is an evolving process.

Write your first draft

For most people, an iterative approach to essay-writing works best. In other words, be prepared to write several drafts. With this in mind we recommend that you:

- Write your essay in any order that you want to – many writers begin with the main body of the essay and leave the introduction until last.
- Write down everything that seems relevant in your first draft and do not censor. You can remove unnecessary material later.
- Do not aim for perfection – leave word crafting until much later in the essay-writing process.

Your first draft should demonstrate the strengths and weaknesses of your position and help to clarify your thinking and understanding. To confirm your own clarity of thought on the issues try summarising your position to a friend or colleague, without referring to your notes. This is a great way to uncover any gaps or 'woolly thinking'.

Develop and refine your essay

We predict that your first draft will include a mix of high- and low-quality writing and content that varies in relevance. You may also have some glaring gaps. You need to continue improving the essay by refining both content and style. Doing this may take a number of iterations – research in this area indicates that 3–4 drafts are common in better student essays. Campbell et al. (1998) found that students who wrote stronger academic essays were more likely to:

- reorganise material across sources when making notes
- engage in continuous drafting of the essay
- revise arguments and ideas not just 'technicalities' such as grammar and spelling.

Be prepared to edit ruthlessly. Although this can feel tedious, each draft will be superior to the previous attempt. Much essay-writing skill lies in what you're prepared to remove!

Continue to check that you are addressing the title

Throughout the writing process refer back to the title. This will avoid the danger of unwittingly 'replacing' the actual title with another and going off at a tangent. You may want to consider using the words in the title to help keep you on track – but remember that too much repetition can be tedious.

Continue to monitor your essay against the marking criteria

As your essay develops check that it meets the marking criteria. How are marks allocated? Does your essay focus on the most important areas?

IT WORKED FOR ME

'When I've finished writing an essay I mark it myself using the marking criteria. I always jot down the mark I would award and the reasons why. Later on I compare my own notes with the teacher's comments. If I'm within 10 marks I celebrate!'

Ask someone uninvolved to read the essay

It is often useful to have your essay looked at by someone unconnected with your course – perhaps a friend from another course? Do they find any sections vague or ambiguous? If so, how can you add precision or clarity? To avoid accusations of cheating and plagiarism, don't share drafts with others in your study group, unless you're all tackling different essays.

Read your essay aloud

We suggest that you read your final draft out loud. This helps to confirm that the overall structure works, as well as providing insight about the flow of individual sentences. At this stage you should not need to make sweeping changes to the content or structure.

Proofread carefully

Proofread a paper copy that you can make notes on. Check the following:

- spelling
- grammar
- references
- length
- adherence to house style (including format and presentation).

Retain electronic and paper copies

Keep a copy of every essay you submit: i) as a back-up if the original goes astray and ii) as a reference for your future study. When you receive your grade and feedback, file it with the essay.

Recognise the rule of diminishing returns

We've described essay writing as an iterative process, which begs the question of when to stop. Anecdotally, it seems that three drafts are typical. Remember that the early revisions are likely to lead to more substantial improvements than later smaller amendments. Try to recognise the point when you are simply 'tweaking' and call it a day. Three or four drafts of an essay are usually enough to secure a reasonable grade.

INTERESTING FINDING

Torrance et al. (2000) identified four undergraduate writing strategies, which they named:

1. **Minimal drafting:** one or two drafts at most.
2. **Outline and develop:** content development before and during drafting.
3. **Detailed planning:** involved techniques such as brainstorming, mindmapping in addition to drafting.
4. **Think-then-do:** preparation without an initial draft.

The 48 students involved in this longitudinal study showed consistency in their chosen methods over time and the students using 'detailed planning' or 'think-then-do' produced better-quality essays than others. Thorough planning is vital.

TOP TIP

Always proofread following an electronic spell-check. Some spelling errors are also genuine words – 'form' instead of 'from' for example – and are not identified by a computer spell-check. One final proofread before submission prevents this happening.

Some of our favourite spell-check gaffes include:

'Freud engaged in extensive seasoning before arriving at his model of . . .'
'There is a rage of thought on this theory . . .'
'The mascara at the Battle of the Somme'
'Evidence is growing in support of global worming'.

4. STRUCTURE: WHAT FORM SHOULD MY ESSAY TAKE?

Academic essays have the following structure:

Title	**How to structure an essay**
Introduction	An introduction follows the title. This is usually one or two paragraphs that interpret the title, state what is (and sometimes what is not) covered within the essay and summarise the key argument. The introduction is the writer's opportunity to set the context by showing how the title has been interpreted and how the subject will be approached.
Key definition?	Key definitions may be included next. The essay should then progress swiftly to the central thesis.
Main body (no subheadings, but clear structure)	The main body of the essay is used to build and develop the central thesis or argument. Every point in the argument should be explored separately, and the supporting and conflicting theory or evidence discussed. (Chapter 10 on critical thinking should help you here.) After discussing the

strengths, weaknesses and alternatives, a conclusion is reached on this aspect of the overall debate. The essay then moves on to the next idea.

Each idea should progress naturally one to another and subheadings are not needed. Instead, the connection between paragraphs is shown by 'signposts' that signal your flow of ideas. These help to ensure that the essay is cohesive and not simply a series of disconnected points. Some examples are shown later in this chapter.

Any quotes must also be structured correctly. Direct quotes should be placed in quotation marks, indented and properly referenced, to avoid plagiarism. Use quotes sparingly and strive to use your own words. As Zinsser (2001) says:

> Remember that words are the only tools you've got. Learn to use them with originality and care.
>
> *(p. 37)*

Conclusion	Finally, after presenting the relevant perspectives there should be a conclusion that pulls together the points made throughout the essay and reconfirms the central argument. At this stage no new ideas or material are introduced.
References Possibly a bibliography	**References** Zinsser, W. (2001) On Writing Well: The Classic Guide to Writing Nonfiction. New York: Harper Resource.

5. STYLE: WHAT KIND OF WRITING SHOULD I USE?

Style relates to your choice and use of language. Just as there is an academic convention around the correct structure of an essay, so there are some conventions around style that the majority of learning organisations have adopted. What aspects of style should you consider when writing an essay?

TRY THIS

Table 11.1 lists eleven aspects of style.

Cover the right-hand column with a piece of paper and then read the topics shown on the left. Before removing the paper, decide what advice you would offer to a new student on each topic.

Table 11.1 Ten aspects of style

Style	Advice
Use of first person	Academic essays have traditionally been written in the third person and have not used the personal pronoun I.
	Sentences such as '**This** essay will explore . . .' rather than '**I** will explore' were considered the norm. More recently this convention has been challenged (e.g. Hamill 1999) and more learning organisations accept both first-and third-person writing. If you're not sure which is acceptable then have a word with your teacher.
	Note that some types of writing, such as reflective journals, may require first-person writing.
	The use of the second person e.g. 'In this essay **you** will discover . . .' is invariably considered poor style.
Tense	Essays tend to be written in the past tense, although there are exceptions. Art and literature, for example, tend to be discussed in the present tense. If you are unsure, ask your tutor which tense is preferred in your subject area.
Gender-specific pronouns	Gender-specific pronouns should be used only when you want to refer specifically to men or to women. Continually repeating words or phrases such as 'he or she' quickly becomes cumbersome. For variety, try using plurals e.g. 'they' or 'people'.
	Only include gender when it's helpful or necessary: e.g. is it relevant that the engineer is 'female'?

Table 11.1 (*cont'd*)

Style	Advice
Using quotes	Direct quotes should be used sparingly, since their over-use prevents you from demonstrating your own understanding. However, they can be effective if well-chosen. If you include direct quotes, then unless they are very short, they should be indented and in inverted commas.
Use of bullet points	Essays should be written using full grammatical sentences, so avoid the use of bullet points or abbreviated sentences.
Voice	Academia traditionally favoured use of the passive voice in essays, but the rules are now more relaxed. For example, take the 'active' sentence 'we are reading this book.' In the passive this becomes 'this book is being read by us.' In the passive voice, the item or person receiving the action is the subject of the sentence and the thing doing the action is optionally included at the end of the sentence. As a general rule, use the active voice unless there is a valid reason for using the passive voice. The main reasons for using passive voice are:

a) You want to emphasise the person or thing being acted upon
   e.g. *Columbus* was ridiculed by his peers.

b) The actor or person 'doing' is not the important point. When writing the experimental methods for a paper, it doesn't usually matter who added the sodium.
   e.g. 20 mg of sodium was added to the solution.

c) The actor is unknown.
   e.g. these cave drawings were painted thousands of years ago.

d) You want to avoid any suggestion of responsibility or blame
   e.g. the animals were killed. Rephrased in the active voice, this becomes 'They/we/somebody killed the animals'.

You can check your understanding of this by completing the activity on page 227.

Table 11.1 *(cont'd)*

Style	Advice
Referencing style	Vancouver and Harvard are the two main referencing styles. Many publications use the Vancouver method which involves numbered references, while learning organisations often use the Harvard approach, which is an alphabetical system. The Harvard system always includes the author and date of publication within the main body of the text, either by writing it into the grammatical structure of the sentence or by including it in brackets. For example:

Smith (1999) investigating classical conditioning in rats found. . .
or
. . . as shown in classical conditioning research involving rats (Smith 1999).

Note that author initials are not included except in the rare case where you cite two different authors with the same surname and with works in the same year. If there are two authors, both names are included e.g. Smith & Brown (2002). When there are three or more authors then only the first author is usually presented in the text e.g. Smith et al. (2004). In the reference list at the end of your text you should always use all the authors' names, no matter how many there are for a given work, and their initials. We've used the Vancouver methods for the interview on sleep (see pages 24–6) and the Harvard system throughout the rest of this book.

Although referencing is not difficult there is little flexibility. That means that you must follow guidelines accurately in order not to lose grades. Learning organisations usually produce their own referencing guide. If you have not seen a copy ask your tutor or librarian how to access one. Remember that all sources should be referenced, e.g. internet or conference sources in addition to journals or books.

| Signposting | Here are some 'signposts' or traditional ways of promoting continuity between one paragraph and the next: |

Table 11.1   *(cont'd)*

Style	Advice
	<ul><li>On the other hand . . .</li><li>As a result of this . . .</li><li>A contrary point of view argues . . .</li><li>Nevertheless . . .</li><li>An alternative approach . . .</li><li>One consequence of this . . .</li><li>Therefore . . .</li><li>Alternatively . . .</li><li>Finally . . .</li><li>However . . .</li></ul>
Language	George Orwell's (1946) advice on language selection generally remains sound:<ul><li>Never use a long word where a short one will do.</li><li>If it is possible to remove a word, always do so.</li><li>Never use a foreign phrase, a scientific word, or a jargon word if you can think of an everyday English equivalent.</li></ul>Why not try the word crafting activity on page 228?
House style	Many learning organisations ask you to use the 'house style'. This is likely to include regulations around:<ul><li>handwritten or typed</li><li>line-spacing requirements e.g. double spaced/single spaced</li><li>margin requirements – some courses request wide margins, or space for comments at the bottom of each page</li><li>style relating to name, personal identifier and course code</li><li>submission format e.g. stapled? plastic folder?</li></ul>
Is there a place for humour?	No, do not try to be funny. Also avoid:<ul><li>colloquial phrases or slang</li><li>sarcasm</li><li>clichés</li><li>over-used metaphors</li><li>rhetorical questions.</li></ul>

TRY THIS

The sentences in the left-hand column are written in the passive voice.
See if you can rewrite them using an active voice. Answers on page 264.

Passive	Active
The exams were taken by the students	The students took the exams
The books were read by the students	The students read the books
The notes are being handed out by the lecturer now	
The sentences in this table should be modified by you	
The theories were presented by the authors	
Your use of the active voice is encouraged by us	

DANGER!

If you write in the first person your reasoning must be
robust and balanced. When writing in the first person it is
easy to slip from objective argument to anecdotal account,
something you need to guard against.

TOP TIP

If your course involves a lot of writing you might want to investigate some of the commercial referencing software that tracks and imports references. Check if your learning organisation has a site licence, or experience of any particular brand first, though.

TRY THIS

See if you can reduce the following passage from 64 words to under 40 without losing any meaning. You are allowed to make changes to the words and the word order, but need to keep the sentiment the same. There are lots of ways to do this, and our 32-word suggestion is on page 264. When you've finished, decide which version you think is easier to read.

> Although I do have a check-list for editing my essays once I've finished writing them, it is not always clear to me how to apply this to my own work. However, I know that one suggestion is to remove any absolutely non-essential words, but I am a little bit worried because I think that may mean my writing ends up much harder to read.

(64 words)

6. ESSAY CONTENT: WHAT SUBJECT MATTER DO I INCLUDE?

The content is the most important aspect of your essay and ensuring high-quality content will draw on all your reading, note-taking and critical thinking skills (see chapters 6, 8 and 10). The questions and answers below deal with some frequent content queries.

Q. *I know a lot about my subject but my essay marks are poor. What am I doing wrong?*

A. Are you receiving comments from markers along the lines of 'don't try to write everything you know' or 'you are answering a different question'? Writing 'everything you know' about a topic does not lead to high grades.

   If you're asked to write an essay but have the freedom to choose your topic within a subject area, the problem may be with your topic selection. So, for example, if you're taking a course in genetics, and you choose to write an essay on 'Cancer', it will be very hard to write a coherent essay unless you narrow the scope. So rather than tackling all aspects of 'Cancer', you could focus on treatments using monoclonal antibodies, or the trigger factors for cell division, or the success of screening programmes for certain types of cancer.

   Your essay must address the question. Always consider carefully what the question is asking and return to the question when writing the essay. You must show how the argument you present in your essay relates to the title. As a result you may need to omit vast amounts of 'what you know' unless it's directly relevant.

   If you find yourself writing phrases such, as 'before addressing the question it is useful to consider', then stop and think. Are you trying to change the question to one that you would prefer? Are you wasting valuable word allowance on irrelevant content?

   Your content must demonstrate your own understanding. You cannot do this if you adhere too closely to the original text or include too many direct quotes. Generally, powerful quotes expressing opinions are acceptable while quotes that outline a theory or model are not required – this is the sort of information that you need to explain in your own words.

Q. *I'm told I spend too long defining terms in my essays. Any suggestions?*

A. This can be a tricky balance to achieve. While it can be dangerous to assume knowledge on the part of the reader, you should not define every term. Keep in mind your intended audience(s) and only define terms that are controversial and/or central to the topic. Use a specialist 'subject' dictionary, and do not try to provide technical definitions using a standard dictionary.

Q. *I'm constantly told that my essays are too descriptive.*

A. A good essay is a logically developed argument or position that considers all sides of the argument. Highly descriptive essays tend not to achieve this. In order to reduce the amount of description, take the time to understand the issues and work out where you stand. This requires good reading and critical thinking skills (chapter 6 and chapter 10).

You need to develop your own position rather than write about a topic. A common misconception about writing is that is it easy. In fact, many people agree that writing well is a difficult skill to acquire, but we can all practise, develop and continue to improve long after we graduate (Robson et al. 2002, Hoadley-Maidment 1997 and Morss & Murray 2001).

> What is written without effort is in general read without pleasure.
>
> *Samuel Johnson*

Q. *I'm worried about plagiarism. When is it acceptable to include the views of others in my essays?*

A. You are not expected to produce new answers to longstanding academic issues and so your essays will always draw on the views of others. What matters is how you do this. Plagiarism is:

- copying, or near-copying, the words of others, without attributing them
- using the ideas of others without attributing them

Plagiarism is considered a serious academic offence and you could fail the essay or even a course if found guilty. To avoid accidental plagiarism you need to write in your own words and reference all ideas that are not your own. Experienced teachers are able to spot plagiarism relatively easily. They are familiar with the key texts, they read many essays and can spot shifting styles that result from plagiarism (Northedge 1990).

Q. *I find it difficult to use subject specific language.*

A. This can be a problem when you are new to a subject. The following ideas may help you:

- Compile a subject glossary, using definitions that are meaningful to you. These days there are many subject dictionaries on the internet so it can be worth reading several definitions.

- Try to familiarise yourself with the technical terms.
- Check your understandings with your teacher or lecturer.

Just as new vocabulary in a foreign language becomes familiar, so do specialist terms. Don't worry if you are clumsy with the new language at first.

IT WORKED FOR ME

'*I try to stick to the principle of the three Cs – Clear, Concise and Connected – when writing and editing. I check that:*

- *my essay is not vague or ambiguous*
- *my sentences are as direct and straightforward as possible*
- *the ideas flow one from another and are connected with the title.*'

7. REVIEW: WHAT CAN I LEARN FOR THE FUTURE?

It is tempting to submit an essay and then forget about it, yet there is a lot that you can learn after submission. Try the suggestions in figure 11.1 (over-leaf) once your essay is returned.

LOOKING AHEAD

Writing expertise comes from practice, so try to view every assignment as an opportunity to develop your writing competency as well as your subject understanding. There is plenty of evidence that good writing skills are important across a range of professions (Evans 1995, Nestel and Kidd 2004, Davies and Birbili 2000). In many jobs, it will be helpful if you can write unambiguous e-mails, clear reports, effective letters, well-argued business cases and balanced appraisals.

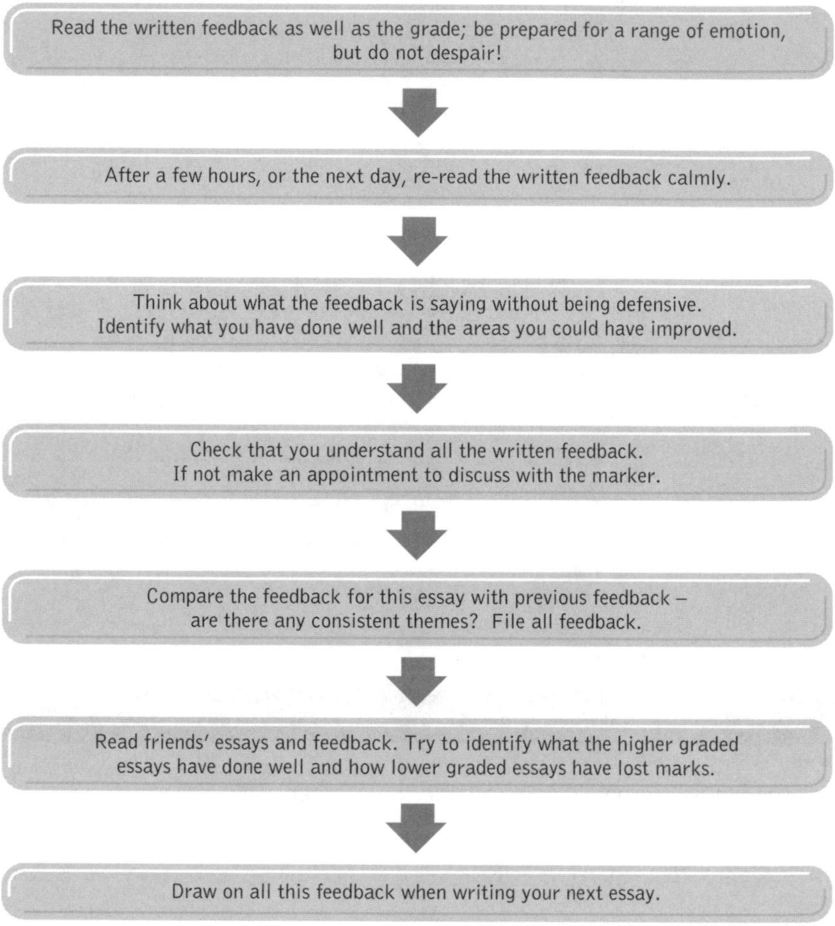

Read the written feedback as well as the grade; be prepared for a range of emotion, but do not despair!

After a few hours, or the next day, re-read the written feedback calmly.

Think about what the feedback is saying without being defensive. Identify what you have done well and the areas you could have improved.

Check that you understand all the written feedback. If not make an appointment to discuss with the marker.

Compare the feedback for this essay with previous feedback – are there any consistent themes? File all feedback.

Read friends' essays and feedback. Try to identify what the higher graded essays have done well and how lower graded essays have lost marks.

Draw on all this feedback when writing your next essay.

Figure 11.1 Dealing with feedback

As a learner you may only be involved in writing essays or you may also be required to submit other written work such as experimental reports, literature reviews or reflective accounts.

We have compared four types of writing in the grid (Table 11.2) opposite – literature reviews, report, reflective accounts and essays. Do you agree with the differences and similarities that we have identified? Is there anything else that you want to add to the grid??

Table 11.2 A comparison of writing types

	Literature review	Reflective account	Research report	Academic essay
Purpose?	Inform (and learn)	Personal development May not have an external audience	Describe and inform (and learn)	Inform (and learn)
Structure?	Longer: 5,000–10,000 words Subheadings, e.g. abstract, introduction	Shorter: 50–1,500 words	Longer: 3,000–5,000 words Subheadings, e.g. method, results.	Shorter: 1,000–3,000 words No subheadings
Style?	Specialist Precise Accurate Balanced	Everyday Colloquial Specialist Precise First person	Specialist Precise Accurate Balanced	Specialist Precise Accurate Balanced
Content?	Analytical Topic often chosen by writer Need to state the criteria used for content selection/inclusion	Descriptive account *plus* analysis Topic chosen by the writer and personal to the writer	Detailed description of methodology plus analysis Restricted choice of title	Analytical Restricted choice of title

SUMMARY

In order to write a good essay you need to focus on several areas (see table below).

Table 11.3 Summary of chapter 11

Purpose	Preparation	Process	Structure	Style	Content	Review
Why?	Allow	Draft	Introduction	Pronouns	Addresses the	Read,
Who?	time to:	Redraft	Main text	Tense	question	understand
What?	Search	Redraft	Conclusion	Gender	Relevant to	and learn
	Read			Quotes	the course	from
	Evaluate			Bullet	No plagiarism	feedback
	Think			points	Clear, concise,	
				Referencing	connected	
				Signposting	Debate not	
				Language	description	
				House style		
				Voice		

12 Portfolios, Reflective Journals and Learning Logs

By three methods we may learn wisdom: first, by reflection, which is noblest; second, by imitation, which is
easiest; and third by experience, which is the bitterest.

Confucius

KEY POINTS

☐ A personal portfolio provides a dynamic record of your learning and development

☐ Reflecting on your own experiences can deliver useful learning

☐ Monitoring your progress against learning objectives encourages self-appraisal

☐ Life-long learning can be a reality for you

INTRODUCTION

This chapter introduces the skill of self-evaluation, which is the application of critical thinking to yourself. Learners and workers are increasingly asked to demonstrate this skill using portfolios, reflective journals and learning logs. The way these terms are defined can vary between organisations, so take care to clarify any formal requirements before beginning.

PORTFOLIOS

. . . . One hot day at the end of June, David flopped onto his bed. It had been a bad week and he felt exhausted. It was the end of his first year at university but instead of feeling relaxed, things seemed to have suddenly gone wrong.

He'd taken his economics exam earlier in the week. This was his favourite subject and he'd expected to do well. Instead, he wasn't even sure that he'd passed.

Then to make matters worse, he had flunked an interview for a summer job. David had expected the interview to be a formality, yet the questions had stumped him. Why had he been asked about his management experience when his application form showed his previous employment to be delivering papers and selling shoes? After all, he would hardly be running the country in his spare time, would he?

He looked at his watch and realised his friends would soon arrive. David was mentally inventing excuses not to go out, when there was a knock on the door and Andrew, Rosie and Amita walked in.

"Hi! Are you ready?"

"Almost," said David.

"What's the matter?" asked Amita, detecting an edge in his voice.

"Nothing," said David.

"It doesn't sound like nothing . . . how did the interview go?"

"Not bad," said David, and then added: "Well, very bad actually! I had a thirty-minute telephone interview and I blew it."

"What went wrong?" asked Andrew.

"Well, for one thing the interviewer asked me questions about my previous positions of responsibility . . ."

"I hope you mentioned being student representative on the hall committee."

David looked sheepish. "I didn't . . . I couldn't think of anything . . . my mind just went blank . . ."

"You need a portfolio," said Rosie. "That would have helped you prepare."

"What's a portfolio?" asked David and Amita together.

"Well," said Rosie, delighted to have everyone's attention, "let me explain . . ."

What is a portfolio?

A personal portfolio is a record of your achievements together with supporting evidence. Brown (1992) described a portfolio as:

> A private collection of evidence which demonstrate the continuing acquisition of skills, knowledge, attitudes, understanding and achievement. It is both retrospective and prospective, as well as reflecting the current stage of development of the individual.

Many formal programmes of study, and some professions, require members to compile a learning portfolio. Guidance is usually provided on the types of evidence that are appropriate. A doctor, for example, might demonstrate involvement in audit projects, research and teaching in addition to therapy specific learning (Driessen et al. 2003).

It is useful to include evidence from all areas of your personal development, even when the portfolio is a formal requirement. In this way you will have a total record of your accomplishments and goals, and you can always remove any highly personal or irrelevant evidence before submitting your portfolio for a formal assessment.

Why keep a personal portfolio?

Reasons for keeping a portfolio include:

1. You have a holistic overview of all your learning and development with readily accessible supporting evidence.
2. It provides an opportunity to identify your own learning strengths, preferences and weaknesses.
3. It provides the motivation to set goals and work towards them systematically.

Do not confuse a portfolio with a CV. A portfolio is a dynamic collection of evidence, while many CVs are little more than a list of job titles and qualifications. Your portfolio might include a copy of your current CV.

LOOKING AHEAD

A well-constructed portfolio demonstrates that you are continuously developing and learning, something that many professions want to see. You can also use your evidence in workplace appraisals and sometimes to gain entry onto learning programmes if you lack formal qualifications, e.g. via Accreditation of Prior Experiential Learning in the UK.

How do I create my portfolio?

The criteria for building a successful portfolio are:

- Include all relevant evidence that demonstrates your personal and professional development.
- Organise, and if need be, cross-reference the evidence.
- Continuously refine and update your portfolio.

The layout of your portfolio depends partly on the type of evidence that you want to include. For example, a learner studying acoustical engineering might include samples of sound recordings, while another studying textiles might incorporate swatches of material. So although your portfolio is likely to be a lever arch file divided into sections, it could also be a suitcase under the bed! Table 12.1 gives examples of some common portfolio inclusions.

TRY THIS

How would you structure your own portfolio?
What evidence would you include?
Where is that evidence currently?

Table 12.1 Common portfolio inclusions

Academic and professional qualifications	Employment record	Positions of responsibility	Hobbies/interests	General achievements	CV and future goals
GCSE certificates	Paper boy – dates and employment record	School prefect – dates and duties	Drama – copies of programmes from amateur dramatic productions	Full driving licence	Current CV
A-level certificates		Representative on university hall committee – dates, responsibilities and achievements, e.g. changing hall menu to healthier options		Excel, Word and PowerPoint IT skills (examples)	Goals: a) 2:1 degree
Undergraduate examination results	Sales assistant – dates and employment record, e.g. sales assistant of the month/handling customer complaints successfully		Chess – list of tournaments and placings		b) trainee risk analyst in the City
Course synopsis		Occasional baby-sitting (include testimonials)	Photography (workshops attended plus examples)		

We all have different experiences to draw on and you should structure your portfolio in the way that is most logical to you. You may, for example, want to demonstrate your achievements as a parent or carer in addition to your formal learning or career accomplishments.

Try to cross-reference your evidence where possible. For example, if you have written a computer program does it demonstrate your problem-solving capability as well as your IT skills?

How easy will it be for you to locate evidence? Do you know where your past examination certificates are right now? Do you have current contact details for past employers or potential referees?

Regard your portfolio as a living document. Update it regularly and check whether past evidence is still useful. For example, evidence from your foundation courses may become less important as your study progresses.

TOP TIP!

 If you are an overseas student, or will be studying abroad, ensure that you compile comprehensive learning evidence as soon as you can. Once you have left a country it can take time and money to collect evidence retrospectively.

Although we have described a portfolio as a collection of evidence, this is a rather simplified description. In order to gain the most benefit from your portfolio you should reflect on the evidence and consider how you can use it in different situations or for different purposes. We look at reflection in more detail in the next section.

. . . . *and so that's what a portfolio is,"* said Rosie, *pausing for breath*.

"If I begin to put a portfolio together would you take a look at it for me?" asked David.

"Of course!"

"Portfolios sound similar to reflective journals," said Andrew, *with studied casualness*.

"What's that?" asked David.

"Well," said Andrew smiling. *"I keep a reflective journal – and I'd say it shares some similarities with your portfolio."*

"Yes, reflective accounts can form part of a portfolio and these may be compulsory if your portfolio is part of an educational or professional require-ment," said Rosie quickly.

"So what is it?" asked the other two.

"Well," said Andrew, *"My sister, who's a teacher, told me about reflective journals when I was telling her about a girlfriend problem."*

The others looked amazed. Andrew typically talked only about football and beer – never relationships!

"You told your sister about a girlfriend problem?" asked David incredulously.

"Under this macho exterior there's a sensitive caring man," Andrew joked.

Rosie and Amita sat up a little straighter.

"Never mind that now," said David. *"What's a reflective journal?"*

REFLECTIVE JOURNALS

The unexamined life is not worth living.

Socrates

What is a reflective journal?

A reflective journal is similar to a diary, in which you describe and then critically appraise your own experiences. The aim is to learn more about your-self through careful analysis and reflection – and this ties in with developing your intrapersonal intelligence (see chapter 3).

In recent years the work of Kolb (1984) (see page 80 for a reminder of Kolb's learning theory) has influenced the use of reflection in education. First you have an experience. Then you reflect on the experience to try and establish why it unfolded as it did. You then think about your role and how you could do things differently to increase or decrease the likelihood of such a situation arising again. In other words, for any experience, you try to figure out what you need to do to avoid, to repeat or to improve a similar sit-uation in the future. You then test those ideas in the real situation and see if

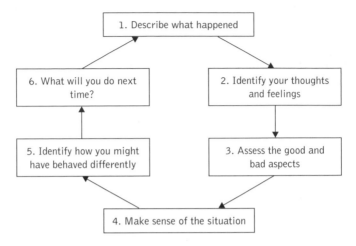

Figure 12.1 Summary of Gibbs' model of reflection

your predictions are met (Imel 1992). Reflection is a sought-after skill both in education and professionally (Dewey 1933, Schon 1983, Harrison et al. 2003, Langer 2002, Ferraro 2000).

There are many models of reflection. Although most follow the same broad outline, the number of individual steps varies. Figure 12.1 shows Gibbs' (1988) model of reflection.

This model demonstrates that when reflecting you must focus on your own thoughts, feelings and behaviours. The aim is to learn from past experiences and plan for future ones.

Why keep a reflective journal?

The benefits of maintaining a reflective journal include:

- Reflective journals offer a safe environment in which to explore your thoughts, feelings and behaviour.
- Reflective journals foster self-awareness and personal growth.
- Reflective journals foster student-centred learning.
- Reflective journals promote critical thinking skills.
  (Jasper cited in Bulman & Schutz 2004)

THINGS TO THINK ABOUT

Do you agree with these benefits?
Can you think of any others?
Are there any disadvantages or barriers?

DANGER!

It can be more difficult to analyse your own motives, thoughts and feelings than it is to pass comment on others!

Keeping a reflective journal may sound simple, yet research suggests:

- New learners may initially write descriptively rather than critically.
- Not everyone finds reflection a 'natural' activity.
- There may be cultural differences in ease of reflection.

(Leung & Kember 2003, Paterson 1995)

A number of important skills are required for successful reflection and these are shown in the mindmap overleaf (figure 12.2):

THINGS TO THINK ABOUT

How many of these skills would
you consider yourself to do well?
How frequently, if ever, are you accused of being defensive?
How easily can you accept that you may be in the wrong?
Are you able to see situations from all perspectives?
Would you say that you deal with your emotions or that you bury them?

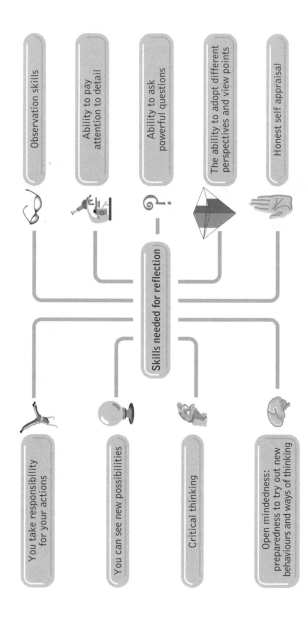

Figure 12.2   Skills needed for reflection

LOOKING AHEAD

Educational, career and life success are about more than collecting certificates. Well-developed interpersonal and intrapersonal skills are increasingly rewarded professionally, and often summed up by the phrase 'emotional intelligence'. Reflection offers an opportunity for you to appraise and improve your own skills in these areas (see also chapter 5).

How do I begin a reflective journal?

Unless you are writing an assessed journal there are no rules around frequency, length or format. You may write as frequently as daily or just once every week or so. We recommend that you try to develop a routine so that reflective writing becomes a study habit.

Similarly there is no recommended length of journal entry, although you may be surprised at the length of your entries for even quite 'simple' events.

While the phrase 'journal' may conjure up images of leather-bound notebooks you can record your reflections on a PC, if that feels more comfortable. We suggest that you consider accessibility by others, and you may decide to password-protect your journal or keep it locked away.

TRY THIS

Think of a time when you have felt bored in a lecture (recently if possible) and reflect upon it using Gibbs' model above. The following questions should be helpful, but do ask any others that you want to.

- **The experience (description):** First describe the situation. What time of day was the lecture? How long was the lecture? Who delivered the lecture? What was the subject and topic? Had you prepared for the lecture? Where were you sitting? Could you see and hear the lecturer? What were you doing? What did you do when you first felt bored?

- **Thoughts and feelings:** What was your physical and mental state at the start of the lecture? What were your expectations about the lecture? Did you view the topic as important? When did you begin to feel bored? How did that affect the learning experience? Did you blame anyone else for your state?

- **Evaluation:** What was good about the situation? Did any aspects fulfil your image of the 'ideal' lecture or the perfect student? What was bad about the situation? Do any of these typify a 'poor' lecture or a 'poor' student?

- **Analysis:** What was happening? What triggered, or contributed to, your feelings of boredom? How do you want to behave and feel in lectures? When do you behave and feel that way?

- **Conclusion:** What could you have done at the time to prevent this situation developing? What can you do to help achieve your desired state? Try to generate different hypotheses, e.g. preparing more beforehand, asking questions in the lecture, arriving on time, eating beforehand, asking friends to stop distracting you , sitting nearer the front, remaining focused? Which of these do you think would have worked best?

- **Action Plan:** What will you do in the future to avoid such a situation developing again? Now do it!

DANGER!

It is very easy to reflect only on negative experiences. Often we take successful experiences for granted and only 'stop and think' when things go wrong. 'Neutral' and 'successful' experiences can also provide important learnings. Why did today go so well?!

TRY THIS

Now choose your own example of a recent experience, and work
through the reflective cycle once more.
How useful did you find this?
What have you learnt?
Will you change your behaviour in the future? How?

IT WORKED FOR ME

'I sometimes return to previous journal entries and re-
analyse them. I've found it useful to consider whether I acted
on my reflections as Intended, or whether I simply repeated
earlier experiences.'

Reflection is about learning for the future. This means that you must test
out your hypotheses in real situations to gain the benefit. Behaving differently (either from the way you have in the past, or differently from others
around you) can be threatening or require personal courage. Yet reflection
cannot be considered successful unless it influences your subsequent behaviour
or changes the way that you feel about the situation (Page & Meerabeau 2000).

"So, today," said David slowly, *"When I was asked in my interview to talk
about positions of responsibility I could have reflected on what I learnt as a
hall representative?"*

"Exactly. And what could you say you've learnt?"

*"Masses about diplomacy, chairing meetings and good timekeeping. I just
wish I'd remembered this before now!"*

*"By keeping a permanent record, either in your portfolio, or reflective
journal, you can remind yourself at any time."*

Amita had been quiet a while but now she spoke up:
"You know, I think this must somehow fit in with learning logs."
"Learning logs?" asked Rosie.
"Yes – written records that show how learning objectives have been met."
"OK – tell us more."

LEARNING LOGS

Learning logs allow you to check that you are meeting the learning objectives set for your course. They are a written record of your performance set against the learning objectives or assessment criteria for your programme of study.

The gold standard for learning objectives is that they should be **SMART**:

Specific: Specific objectives are unambiguous – there is no dispute about what is required. An example might be learning the periodic table by rote.

Measurable: You can demonstrate that a measurable objective has been met, e.g. reproduce an error-free periodic table without using aids.

Acceptable: Acceptable objectives have relevant outcomes set at the correct level, e.g. memorising the periodic table is a requirement of the undergraduate chemistry programme.

Realistic: Realistic objectives are feasible, e.g. undergraduate students are capable of learning the periodic table.

Time-bound: Time-bound objectives must be met within a defined time, e.g. periodic table must be learnt within the first semester.

TRY THIS

1. Take a look at the learning objectives that accompany your course. Are they all SMART? If not do you need to ask for any additional clarification?

2. Pick a topic that you have recently explored and see if you can set a SMART learning objective. For example, one SMART objective when reading this book might be: At the end of this chapter you will be able to identify and define all five criteria for SMART learning objectives.

This is a very simple or low-level learning objective. Higher-level or applied learning objectives typically require more consideration in deciding how and when they've been met.

It is easier to assess your own performance against learning objectives when they are in a SMART format. Table 12.2 is an example of a simple learning log.

As you can see, a learning log can literally be a list of learning objectives with space for you to record when and how you met the requirements of each. Spaces show where any outstanding gaps in achievement.

Table 12.2 A simple learning log

Learning objective	How I've met the objective/evidence	Date achieved
List and describe the function of the eight major endocrine glands (By xx)	Submitted an 'A' grade assignment on the function of the eight major endocrine glands	1 March 2005
Critically review the methodology of a research article published in the Journal of xx (By xx) Describe the assessment and treatment of one endocrine disorder (By xx)	Attended research awareness modules at the end of which I presented a critical review of article xxx in a seminar – received excellent feedback	24 May 2005

THINGS TO THINK ABOUT

Do you have learning objectives for
your present programme of study?
How do you use the objectives?

Learning logs offer a record of what you've learnt and can also help you to:

* monitor your progress
* plan your study
* make the syllabus manageable
* work towards particular learning objectives.

TRY THIS

Set up and use a learning log for your next module or programme of study.

At the end of the module reflect on the experience. Did the learning log help you to learn more effectively?

FREQUENTLY ASKED QUESTIONS

Q. *I've been reading round and have found several, slightly different, descriptions of learning logs, portfolios and reflective diaries.*

A. Yes, we have separated the three tools here for simplicity, although they can overlap. Learning logs may include reflective accounts or evidence, for example. If portfolios, reflective journals or learning logs form part of your course requirements, ensure that you understand their precise role and the assessment criteria.

Q. *How much evidence is there that such tools are effective – in either the short or longer term?*

A. The literature contains a range of views. Many are based on theory rather than research. Pertinent research is typically small scale and not longitudinal, and outcome measures tend to focus on users' perceptions, rather than measuring learning or performance improvements (Cornford 2002). However, respondents do find the tools valuable (though not necessarily simple to use) and believe them to enhance their personal or professional development.

   The tools support current educational philosophies including Life Long Learning and Student Focused Learning. We are advocating them for personal use on the basis of the literature and the common-sense platform that these tools provide visible evidence of your own achievements, and incorporate many of the principles we already know about effective learning.

Q. *This all sounds like it's adding to my workload rather than reducing it.*

A. Portfolios and reflection, in particular, should save you time when applying for jobs or further study. A learning log should help you to organise your study time effectively and again, can help you develop insights into your own natural aptitudes.

Q. *Do I need to reflect by myself or can I reflect with others?*

A. Either. If you reflect alone you may be restrained by your own world biases or any reluctance to explore issues fully or honestly. On the other hand reflection with others can be difficult due to the limitations of language and the potential for misinterpretation, or because of issues around exposure. You will need a safe environment, with high levels of trust to avoid embarrassment and censorship.

Q. *I have to keep a reflective journal as a course requirement but the prospect of somebody else reading it is making it hard for me to be honest.*

A. Check how your tutors will use the journal. It may be that you will be able to choose an entry to read or discuss, and therefore have choice over what you disclose.

SUMMARY

This chapter described three tools that you can use to monitor you learning:

Learning record	Principal role
Learning portfolio	Records your total learning achievements
Reflective journal	Records your learning from experience
Learning log	Records your progress against learning objectives

The uses of all three tools can overlap. Drawing on these concepts will help you to be a Life Long Learner.

POSTSCRIPT

David scraped through his first-year economics exam and spent that summer at his local supermarket checkout, learning how to handle boredom and difficult customers. Two years, one portfolio and many learning objectives later he graduated with a 2:1 degree.

Next Steps

The *Smart Study Guide* has explored many aspects of effective study. The *Smart Study Guide* is most useful if you:

- review the information
- apply the relevant information every time you study
- monitor the contribution this makes to your learning effectiveness
- set yourself learning goals to help fulfil your learning potential.

We recommend two 'next steps'.

Step 1. Consider how *The Smart Study Guide* has already contributed to your study effectiveness. If you can already see a difference then is that additional motivation to continue drawing on the information contained here? You may find these questions below helpful for this exercise:

Q. Has this book already affected the way you perceive, or approach, any of the following?

- your motivation to learn
- yourself as a learner
- your strengths and abilities
- your potential
- how you prepare for study
- the way you read
- working with other learners

- the quality of your notes
- learning by rote
- evaluating academic theories
- evaluating academic research
- the quality of your essays
- time spent on activities such as this!

Q. Where do you think your biggest learning gains have been?

Q. Which chapter(s) would you gain most benefit from reading again?

Q. What study behaviours have you already changed?

Q. Where are your greatest opportunities for becoming a more effective learner?

Q. What do you need to do now?

Step 2. In order to maximise the benefits you gain try to incorporate our suggestions into your study routine, by doing the following:

Reviewing: To help you review the material, we have summarised the overall content in the diagrams on pages 255 and 256. Why not add any points that you found particularly helpful?

Applying: At the beginning of every learning activity, decide which material is relevant and afterwards ask yourself:

- Did I make use of the material?
- Which material did I use?
- How did I use that material?

Monitoring: How did the information contribute to your learning effectiveness? What will you do differently next time? What will you repeat next time?

Setting goals: Try to set yourself goals that will stretch you as a learner. Rather than settle for being good enough, why not try to see how good a learner you can be?

Finally, we hope you find The Smart Study Guide useful. The following mindmaps give an overview of the chapters. We would love to hear your feedback and experiences. You can e-mail us at louise&pat@smartstudyguide.com

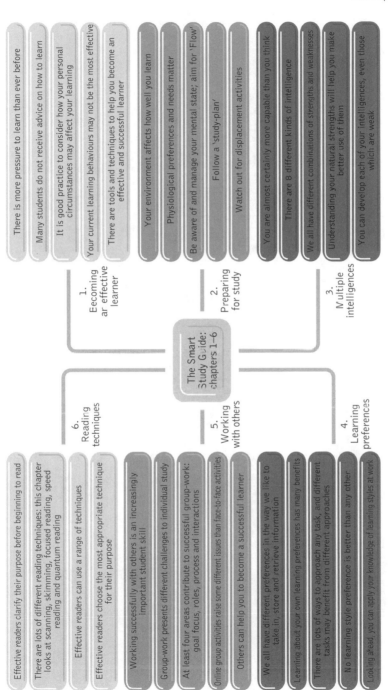

There is more pressure to learn than ever before

Many students do not receive advice on how to learn

It is good practice to consider how your personal circumstances may affect your learning

Your current learning behaviours may not be the most effective

There are tools and techniques to help you become an effective and successful learner

1. Becoming an effective learner

Your environment affects how well you learn

Physiological preferences and needs matter

Be aware of and manage your mental state; aim for 'Flow'

Follow a 'study-plan'

Watch out for displacement activities

2. Preparing for study

You are almost certainly more capable than you think

There are 8 different kinds of intelligence

We all have different combinations of strengths and weaknesses

Understanding your natural strengths will help you make better use of them

You can develop each of your intelligences, even those which are weak

3. Multiple intelligences

The Smart Study Guide: chapters 1–6

Effective readers clarify their purpose before beginning to read

There are lots of different reading techniques: this chapter looks at scanning, skimming, focused reading, speed reading and quantum reading

Effective readers can use a range of techniques

Effective readers choose the most appropriate technique for their purpose

6. Reading techniques

Working successfully with others is an increasingly important student skill

Group-work presents different challenges to individual study

At least four areas contribute to successful group-work: goal focus, roles, process and interactions

Online group activities raise some different issues than face-to-face activities

Others can help you to become a successful learner

5. Working with others

We all have different preferences in the way we like to take in, store and retrieve information

Learning about your own learning preferences has many benefits

There are lots of ways to approach any task, and different tasks may benefit from different approaches

No learning style preference is better than any other

Looking ahead, you can apply your knowledge of learning styles at work

4. Learning preferences

Figure A1 Overview of chapters 1–6

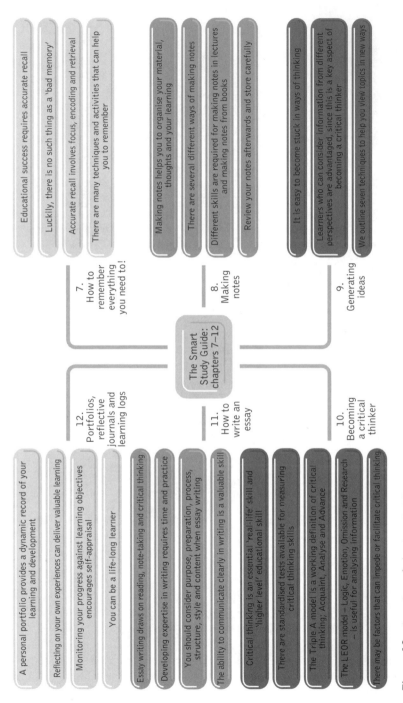

Figure A2   Overview of chapters 7–12

Appendix 1 Gardner's Criteria for Intelligence

Gardner (1999) suggests that in order for an ability to be considered an 'intelligence', it needs to meet the following eight criteria 'reasonably well', taking into account evidence from brain research, human development, evolution, and cross-cultural comparisons. The criteria are:

- **Experience of idiot savants, prodigies and other exceptional individuals.** Although rare, there will be some individuals who have a 'truly exceptional' ability in the intelligence, which was evident at a young age; e.g. Mozart's musical performances at the age of 4.
- **An identifiable core set of operations**. True intelligences will have basic kinds of information-processing operations or mechanisms that deal with one specific kind of input.
- **A distinctive developmental history**. A true intelligence has an identifiable set of stages of growth with a 'Mastery level' which exists as an end state in human development. For true intelligences, there will be examples of people who have reached the Mastery level.
- **An evolutionary history and evolutionary plausibility**. It is generally accepted among anthropologists and evolutionary biologists that our species developed intelligence over time. For true intelligences, there will be evidence of this evolutionary development and plausible explanations.
- **Support from experimental and psychological tasks**. A true intelligence can be identified by specific tasks which can be carried out, observed and measured by clinical psychologists.
- **Support from psychometric findings**. Traditionally, psychometric instruments have been used to measure intelligence (e.g. IQ tests). Such tests could be designed and used to identify and quantify true unique intelligences. The Multiple

Intelligence theory does not reject psychometric testing for specific scientific study.

- **Potential isolation by brain damage**. The functioning of a true intelligence will be location in specific areas of the brain. Research involves studies of brain injury and degenerative diseases.
- **Susceptibility to encoding from a symbol system**. Humans have developed many kinds of symbol systems over time for varied disciplines. A true intelligence has its own set of images or symbols, which are unique to itself and are important in completing its identified set of tasks.

Page 58: Crossword answers (Example 3)

Across:
5. INTRAPERSONAL
6. SPATIAL
7. NATURALIST
8. INTERPERSONAL

Down:
1. MUSICAL
2. KINAESTHETIC
3. VERBAL
4. MATHEMATICAL

Page 117: Question types (Table 6.2)

	Relevance	Prediction	Challenge	Fact/Opinion	Associate	Explain
How can I apply this to x	✓					
Where's the author going with this		✓				
How do we know this is true			✓	✓		
What are the other possible explanations			✓		✓	✓
What do we know since this was published				✓		
What is the author going to conclude		✓				
How reliable is the evidence			✓	✓		
What evidence supports the claim				✓		
Where else was this presented					✓	
How would I explain this to x						✓

Page 127: Scan, skim or focus

1. I need to confirm the percentage of smokers under the age of 25.

    <u>Scan</u> **Skim** **Focus**

2. I'm going on a field trip to China next month and want to buy a travel guide. There are 3 books on the shelf, and I don't know which one to choose.

    Scan **<u>Skim</u>** **Focus**

3. I need to prepare a 90 minute presentation explaining this author's main ideas.

    Scan **Skim** **<u>Focus</u>**

4. I've been asked to critique this research article.

    Scan **Skim** **<u>Focus</u>**

5. I'm trying to decide whether to take this course next semester. The material for each week is based on a different chapter from this textbook.

    Scan **<u>Skim</u>** **Focus**

6. I'm revising for my exams, and need to check what year a particular study was published.

    <u>Scan</u> **Skim** **Focus**

Page 186: Our thought bubbles . . .

'This is the ideal car for you.'

Mmm ...bet he says that to everyone...... wonder what he means by ideal .... I'll try to pin him down on that...

'It's been exceptionally well looked after. Only one careful owner since new and it has been serviced regularly.'

I'll check the vehicle registration document to see how many owners.... and ask to see the service record..if he doesn't have it then how does he know?

'Not only is this car a great little goer, but it's just been fitted with new tyres and a new clutch.'

I'll check the tread on each tyre in a moment... now how can I find out about the clutch....?

'It does 35 mpg and this model is renowned for its reliability. I'd strongly recommend that you give it a test drive – it's bound to sell quickly!'

I'll take a look at the manufacturers' information and see what mpg they say...

Page 214: Sample guide to marking essays

If you are grading essays without any specific marking criteria, then we suggest that you consider the following areas. Our suggested 'weightings' are also shown.

Well presented and correctly referenced – 0–5%

Is the referencing format correct?

Are all the references included?

Is the 'house style' met?

Writing style – 0–10%

Is it grammatical?

Are the sentences well constructed?

Content – 0–45%

Is this content relevant?

Does the content demonstrate understanding?

Are there any areas of confusion? Or inaccuracies?

Are there any important omissions?

Is information from different sources synthesised?

Critical appraisal/evaluation 0–40%

Is the topic critically appraised and evaluated?

Does the essay present and discuss different points of view?

How coherent, insightful or sophisticated are the arguments presented?

Is there any originality in the arguments expressed, the examples used or the applications suggested?

Page 227: Active/Passive voice

Passive	Active (include the first two as examples)
The exams were taken by the students	The students took the exams
The books were read by the students	The students read the books
The notes are being handed out by the lecturer now	*The lecturer is handing out the notes now*
The sentences in this table should be modified by you	*You should modify the sentences in this table*
The theories were presented by the authors	*The authors presented their theories*
Your use of the active voice is encouraged by us	*We encourage you to use the active voice*

Page 229: Word Crafting

I have a check-list for editing finished essays, but struggle to apply it. One suggestion is to remove non-essential words, but I worry in case it makes my writing harder to read.

(32 words)

References

WEBSITE REFERENCES

Topic	Website
New Buildings Institute website (chapter 2)	www.newbuildings.org
Multiple Intelligences: Howard Gardner's Project Zero website (chapter 3)	www.pz.harvard.edu
Multiple Intelligence Developmental Assessment Scales (MIDAS) website (chapter 3)	www.miresearch.org
The Honey & Mumford Learning Style questionnaire (chapter 4)	www.peterhoney.co.uk/ls80.
Learning styles analysis for adults, (including environmental and physical preferences) (chapter 4)	www.learningstyles.com
Belbin's group roles and teamworking (chapter 5)	www.belbin.com/
Speed reading (chapter 6)	www.speedyreader.co.uk
Logical fallacies (chapter 10)	www.fallacyfiles.org/.
Logical fallacies (chapter 10)	www.adamsmith.org/logicalfallacies/

BOOKS AND ARTICLES

Adair, J. 1989. *Effective Team Building*. London: Gower.

Adams, R. S., Turns, J. & Atman, C. J. 2003. Educating effective engineering designers: The role of reflective practice. *Design Studies*, vol. 24, no. 3, pp. 275–294.

Ajraktarevic, N., Hall, W. & Fullick, P. 2003. Incorporating learning styles in hypermedia environment: Empirical evaluation. *Workshop on Adaptive Hypermedia and Adaptive Web-Based Systems*. Twelfth International World Wide Web Conference, Budapest, Hungary, 20 May 2003. Retrieved on 29 Apr. 2004 from: wwwis.win.tue.nl/ah2003/proceedings

Alty, J. L., Knott, R. P., Anderson, B. & Smyth, M. 2000. A framework for engineering metaphor at the user interface. *Interacting with Computers*, vol. 13, pp. 301–322.

Andrusyszyn, M. A. & Davie, L. E. 1995. Reflection as a tool in computer mediated education. Presented at: Distance Education Conference, San Antonio, Texas. Retrieved on 12 May 2004 from: www.oise.utoronto.ca/~Idavie/reflect.html

Argyle, M. 1994. *The Psychology of Social Class*. London: Routledge.

Austin, J. L., Lee, M. & Carr, J. P. 2004. The effects of guided notes on undergraduate students' recording of lecture content. *Journal of Instructional Psychology*, vol. 31, issue 4 pp. 314–320.

Ausubel, D. 1968. *Educational Psychology: A Cognitive View*, New York: Holt, Rinehart & Winston.

Back, M., Cohen, J., Harrison, S. & Minneman, S. 2002. Speeder Reader: An experiment in the future of reading. *Computers & Graphics*, vol. 26, no. 4, pp. 623–627.

Bacon J. 2001. Tutoring and mentoring online. Briefing Paper N. 20. JISC. Retrieved on 29 Apr. 2004 from: www.jisc.ac.uk/index.cfm?name=mle_briefings_20

Baddeley, A. D. 1999. *Essentials of Human Memory*. Hove, Sussex: Psychology Press Limited.

Badia, P., Myers, B., Boecker, M., Culpepper, J. & Harsh, J. R. 1991. Bright light effects on human body temperature, alertness, EEG, and behavior. *Physiology and Behavior*, vol. 50, no. 3, pp. 583–588.

Ballone, L. M. & Czerniak, C. 2001. Teachers' beliefs about accommodating students' learning styles in science classes. *Electronic Journal of Science Education*, vol. 6, no. 2, Article Three. Retrieved on 12 May 2004 from: unr.edu/homepage/crowther/ejse/balloneetal.pdf

Battista, Michael T. 1999. The mathematical miseducation of America's youth. Retrieved on 29 Sep. 2004 from: www.pdkintl.org/kappan/kbat9902.htm

Belbin, R. M. 2003. *Management Teams: Why They Succeed or Fail*. 2nd edn, Oxford: Butterworth, Heinemann.

Berge, Z. L. 1995. Facilitating computer conferencing: Recommendations from the field. *Education Technology*, vol. 35, no. 1, pp. 22–30.

Biggers, J. L. 1980. Body rhythms, the school day, and academic achievement. *Journal of Experimental Education*, vol. 49, no. 1, pp. 45–47.

Bion, W. R. 1961. *Experiences in Groups and Other Papers*. London: Tavistock.

Black, S. 1997. The musical mind. *American School Board Journal*, January, pp. 20–22.

Blasko, D. G. 1999. Only the tip of the iceberg: Who understands what about metaphor? *Journal of Pragmatics*, vol. 31, pp. 1675–1683.

Bloom, B. S. (ed.) 1956. *Taxonomy of Educational Objectives: The Classification of Educational Goals: Handbook I, Cognitive Domain*. New York/Toronto: Longmans, Green.

Boud, D. 2001. Using journal writing to enhance reflective practice. In L. M. English & M. A. Gillen (eds), Promoting journal writing in adult education, *New Directions in Adult and Continuing Education*, no. 90, pp. 9–18.

Boud, D., Keogh, R. & Walker, D. (eds) 1985. *Reflection: Turning Experience into Learning*. London: Kogan Page.

Bourner, J., Hughes, M. & Bourner, T. 2001. First year undergraduate experiences of group work. *Assessment and Evaluation in Higher Education*, vol. 26, no. 1, pp. 19–39.

Boyle, E. A., Duffy, T. & Dunleavy, K. 2003. Learning styles and academic outcome: The validity and utility of Vermunt's Inventory of Learning Styles in a British higher education setting. *British Journal of Educational Psychology*, vol. 73, no. 2, pp. 267–90.

Bridgett, D. J. & Cuevas, J. 2000. Effects of listening to Mozart and Bach on the performance of a mathematical test. *Perceptual and Motor Skills*, vol. 90, no. 3, pp. 1171–1175.

Brigden, D. 1999. Constructing a learning portfolio. *British Medical Journal*, vol. 319, no. 7201, pp. 2–3.

Brindley, C. & Scoffield, S. 1998. Peer assessment in undergraduate programmes. *Teaching in Higher Education*, vol. 3, no. 1 pp. 79–90.

Brooks, C. M. & Ammons, J. L. 2003. Free Riding in group projects and the effects of timing, frequency and specificity of criteria in peer assessments. *Journal of Education for Business,* May/June, pp. 268–272.

Brown, R. A. 1992. *Profile Development and Profiling for Nurses*. Lancaster: Quay Publishing.

Brown, R. & McNeil, D. 1966. The 'tip of the tongue' phenomenon. *Journal of Verbal Learning and Verbal Behaviour*, vol. 5, pp. 325–337.

Browne, M. N. & Keeley, S. M. 2004. *Asking the Right Questions: A Guide to Critical Thinking*. New Jersey: Pearson Education.

Butcher, A. C., Stefani, L. A. J. & Tariq, V. N. 1995. 'Analysis of peer, self and staff assessment in project work assessment in education: Principles *Policy & Practice*, vol. 2, Issue 2, pp. 165–185.

Buzan, T. 1993. *The Mind Map Book*. New York: Dutton.

Buzan, T. 2003. *Use Your Memory*. London: BBC Books.

Callan, R. J. 1998. Giving students the (right) time of day. *Educational Leadership*, vol. 55, no. 4, pp. 84–87.

Campbell, D. 1997. *The Mozart Effect*. Chatham, Kent: Hodder & Stoughton.

Campbell, J., Smith, D. & Brooker, R. 1998. From conception to performance: How undergraduate students conceptualise and construct essays. *Higher Education*, vol. 36, pp. 449–469.

Carrier, C. A., 1983. Note taking research: Implications for the classroom. *Journal of Instructional Development*, vol. 6, no. 3, pp. 19–25.

Carskadon, M. A., Wolfson, A. R., Acebo, C., Tzischinsky, O. & Seifer, R. 1998. Adolescent sleep patterns, circadian timing, and sleepiness at a transition to early school days. *Sleep*, vol. 21, no. 8, pp. 871–881.

Carver, R. P. 1985. How good are some of the world's best readers? *Reading Research Quarterly*, vol. 20, pp. 389–419.

Cash, C. S., Earthman, G. I. & Van Berkum, D. 1996. Student achievement, behavior & school building condition. *Journal of School Business Management*, vol. 8, no. 3, p. 26.

Cassaday, H. J., Bloomfield, R. E. & Hayward, N. 2002. Relaxed conditions can provide memory cues in both undergraduates and primary school children. *British Journal of Educational Psychology*, vol. 72, pp. 531–547.

Checkley, K. 1997. 'Teaching for Multiple Intelligences: The First Seven . . . and the Eighth: A Conversation with Howard Gardner *Education Leadership*, vol. 55, no. 1, pp. 8–13.

Cheng, Y. C. 1994. Classroom environment and student affective performance: An effective profile. *Journal of Experimental Education*, vol. 62, no. 3, pp. 221–240.

Cheung, C. K., Rudowicz, E., Lang, G., Yue, X. D. & Kwan, A. S. F. 2001. Critical thinking among university students: Does the family background matter?' *College Student Journal*, vol. 35, no. 4, pp. 577–598.

Chew, M. K. & Laubichler, M. D. 2003. Natural Enemies – Metaphor or Misconception? *Science*, vol. 301, no. 5629, pp. 52–53.

Chung, S. T. L., Legge, G. E. & Cheung, S. H. 2004. Letter–recognition and reading speed in peripheral vision benefit from perceptual learning. *Vision Research*, vol. 44, no. 7, pp. 695–709.

Cockerton, T., Moore, S. & Norman, D. 1997. Cognitive test performance and background music. *Perpetual and Motor Skills*, vol. 85, pp. 1435–1438.

Coffield, F., Moseley, D. Hall, E. & Ecclestone, K. 2004a. *Should We Be Using Learning Styles? What Research Has To Say To Practice*. London: Learning and Skills Research Centre/University of Newcastle upon Tyne.

Coffield, F. J., Moseley, D. V., Hall, E. & Ecclestone, K. 2004b. *Learning Styles and Pedagogy in Post-16 Learning: A Systematic and Critical Review*. London: Learning and Skills Research Centre/University of Newcastle upon Tyne.

Cook, K. 2000. First class primer for CMC courses. Retrieved 3 Oct. 2004 from: fcis.oise.utoronto.ca/%7Ekcook/fcprimer.htm

Cook, M. J. in press. An exploratory study of learning styles as a predictor of college academic adjustment. *Fairfield University Student Psychology Journal*. Retrieved 12 March 2006 from: www.matthewjcook.com/research/cv.html. Retrieved 02 Jun. 2004 from: www.matthewjcook.com/research/learnstyle.pdf

Cornford, I. R. 2002. Reflective teaching: Empirical research findings and some implications for teacher education. *Journal of Vocational Education and Training*, vol. 54, no. 2, pp. 219–235.

Crawford, C. C. 1925. Some experimental studies of the results of college note-taking. *Journal of Educational Research*, vol. 12, pp. 379–386.

Crowder, R. G. & Wagner, R. W. 1992. *The Psychology of Reading: An Introduction*. New York: Oxford University Press.

Csikszentmihalyi, M. 2002. *Flow. The Classic Work on How to Achieve Happiness*. London: Rider and Co.

Cuthbert, K. 2001. Independent study and project work: Continuities or discontinuities. *Teaching in Higher Education*, vol. 6, no. 1, pp. 69–84.

Davies, C. & Birbili, M. 2000. What do people need to know about writing in order to write in their jobs? *British Journal of Educational Studies*, vol. 48, no. 4, pp. 429–445.

Davis, M. 2003. Barriers to reflective practice: The changing nature of higher education. *Active Learning in Higher Education*, vol. 4, no. 3, pp. 243–255.

Dearing, R. 1997. *Report of the National Committee of Inquiry into Higher Education: Higher Education in a Learning Society*. London: HMSO. Retrieved on 17 Aug. 2005 from: www.leeds.ac.uk/educol/ncihe

DeBono, E. 1986. *Six Thinking Hats*. New York: Little Brown.

De Vries, K. 2002. Teaching to their strengths: Multiple intelligence theory in the college writing class. Unpublished PhD dissertation, University of Massachusetts, Amherst.

Dewey, J. 1933. *How we think*. New York: D. C. Heath.

Dilts, R., 1977. EEG and representational systems. In *Roots of NLP*, Meta Publications (1983). Retrieved on 4 Oct. 2004 from: www.nlpu.com/research.htm

DiPetta T. 1998. Type as a facilitation tool in computer conferencing. In P. Cranton, (ed.), *Psychological Type in Action*. Sneedville, TN: Psychological Type Press. Abridged version retrieved on 5 Feb. 2004 from: node.on.ca/tfl/notes/dipetta.html

Dochy, F., Segers, M., Van den Bossche, P. & Gijbels, D. 2003. Effects of problem-based learning: A meta-analysis. *Learning and Instruction*, vol. 13, pp. 533–568.

Doyle, M. & Garland, J. 2001. A course to teach cognitive and affective learning strategies to university students. *Guidance and Counselling*, vol. 16, no. 3, pp. 86–92.

Driessen, E. W., VanTartwijk, J., Vermunt, J. D. & Van Der Vleuten, C. P. M. 2003. Use of portfolios in early undergraduate medical training. *Medical Teacher*, vol. 25, no. 1, pp. 18–23.

Drysdale, M., Ross, J. & Schulz, R. 2001. Cognitive learning styles and academic performance in 19 first-year university courses: Successful students versus students at risk. *Journal of Education for Students Placed at Risk*, vol. 6, no. 3, pp. 271–289.

Dunn, R. & Dunn, K. J. 1979. Learning styles/teaching styles: Should they, can they be matched? *Educational Leadership*, vol. 36, pp. 238–244.

Dunn, R., Della Valle, J., Dunn, K., Geisert, G., Sinatra, R. & Zenhausern, R. 1986. The effects of matching and mismatching students' mobility preferences on recognition and memory tasks. *Journal of Educational Research*, vol. 79, no. 5., pp. 267–272.

Earthman, G. I. 2002. *School Facility Conditions and Student Achievement*. Los Angeles: IDEA, UCLA. Retrieved on 15 Aug. 2005 from: www.idea.gseis.ucla.edu/publications/williams/reports/pdfs/wws08-Earthman.pdf

Ennis, R. H. & Millman, J. 1985. *Cornell Critical Thinking Test, Level X*. Pacific Grove, CA: Midwest Publications.

ERIC Digest 1998. Critical thinking skills and teacher education. *ERIC Digest 3–88*. Retrieved 1 March 2006 from: www.ericdigests.org/pre-929/critical.htm.

ERIC Digest 1990. Developing Metacognition. *ERIC Digest*. Retrieved 1 March 2006 from: www.ericdigests.org/pre-929/critical.htm.

Evans, G. & Johnson, D. 2000. Stress and open-office noise. *Journal of Applied Psychology*, vol. 85, no. 5, pp. 779–783.

Evans, M. D. 1995. Student and faculty guide to improved technical writing. *Journal of Professional Issues in Engineering Education and Practice*, vol. 121, no. 2, 114–122.

Facione, P. A. 1990. The California Critical Thinking Skills Test. College Level Technical Report No. 1, *Experimental Validation and Content Validity*, ERIC Document ED 327-549. Retrieved 12 March 2006 from: www.insightassessment.com/articles3.html.

Felner, R. D., Brand, S., DuBois, D. L., Adan, A. M., Mullhall, P. F. & Evans, E. G. 1995. Socioeconomic disadvantage, proximal environmental experiences and socioemotional and academic adjustment in early adolescence: Investigation of mediated effects model. *Child Development*, vol. 66, pp. 774–792.

Fernandes, C. J. & Speer, M. E. 2002. Using mnemonics and visual imagery to teach the new neonatal resuscitation program. *Journal of Perinatology*, vol. 22, pp. 411–413.

Fernandez-Duque, D. & Johnson, M. 1999. Attention metaphors: How metaphors guide the cognitive psychology of attention. *Cognitive Science,* vol. 23, no. 1, pp. 83–116.

Ferraro, J. M. 2000. Reflective practice and professional development. *ERIC Digest*. Retrieved 1 March 2006 from: www.ericdigests.org/2001-3/reflective.html.

Flavell, J. H. 1976. Metacognitive aspects of problem solving. In L. B. Resnick (ed.), *The Nature of Intelligence*, pp. 231–236. Hillsdale, NJ: Erlbaum.

Freeman, M. 2001. Reflective logs: An aid to clinical teaching and learning. *International Journal of Language and Communication Disorders*, vol. 36, pp. 411–416.

Gadzella, B. M., Ginther, D. W. & Bryant, G. W. 1997. Prediction of performance in an academic course by scores on measures of learning style and critical thinking. *Psychological Reports*, vol. 81, pp. 595–602.

Gardner, H. 1983. *Frames of Mind: The Theory of Multiple Intelligences*. New York: Basic Books.

Gardner, H. 1991. *Intelligence in Seven Steps in Creating the Future: Perspectives on Educational Change* (ed. Dee Dickinson). Seattle: New Horizons.

Gardner, H. 1995. Reflections on multiple intelligences: Myths and messages. *Phi Delta Kappan,* vol. 77, no. 3, pp. 200–209

Gardner, H. 1999. *Intelligence Reframed: Multiple Intelligences for the 21st Century*. New York: Basic Books.

Gersick, C. J. G. 1988. Time and transition in work teams: Toward a new model of group development. *Academy of Management Journal*, vol. 31, pp. 9–41.

Gibbs, G. 1998. *Learning by Doing: A Guide to Teaching and Learning Methods*. London: FEU.

Gomes, L., Martinho, P., Castelo Branco, A. & Castelo Branco, N. 1999. Effects of occupational exposure to low-frequency noise on cognition. *Aviation, Space, and Environmental Medicine*, vol. 70, no. 3, Section 2 (suppl.), pp. A 115–118.

Halpern, D. F. 1995. *Thought and Knowledge: An Introduction to Critical Thinking*. Mahwah, NJ: Lawrence Erlbaum Associates.

Hamill, C. 1999. Academic essay writing in the first person: A guide for undergraduates. *Nursing Standard*, vol. 13, no. 44, pp. 38–40.

Hancock, P. A. & Vasmatzidis, I. 2003. Effects of heat stress on cognitive performance: The current state of knowledge. *International Journal of Hyperthermia*, vol. 19: 355–372.

Harner, D. P. 1974. The effects of thermal environments on learning skills. *Educational Facility Planner*, vol. 12, no. 2, pp. 4–6.

Harrison, M., Short, C. & Roberts, C. 2003. Reflecting on reflective learning: The case of geography, earth and environmental sciences. *Journal of Geography in Higher Education*, vol. 27, no. 2, pp. 133–152.

Harrison, Y. & Young, J. A. 1997. Sleep deprivation effects speech. *Sleep*, vol. 20, no. 10, pp. 871–877.

Harrison, Y. & Young, J. A. 1998. Sleep loss impairs short and novel language tasks having a prefontal focus. *Journal of Sleep Research*, vol. 7, pp. 95–100.

Harrison, Y. & Young, J. A. 1999. One night of sleep loss impairs innovative thinking and flexible decision making. *Organizational Behavior and Human Decision Process*, vol. 7, pp. 128–145.

Harrison, Y. & Young, J. A. 2000. Sleep loss and temporal memory. *Quarterly Journal of Experimental Psychology*, vol. 53A, no. 1, pp. 271–279.

Hathaway, W. 1988. Educational facilities: Neutral with respect to learning and human performance. *CEFPI Journal*, vol. 26, no. 4, pp. 8–12.

Hays, J. R. & Vincent, J. P. 2004, Students' evaluations of problem-based learning in graduate psychology courses. *Teaching of Psychology*, vol. 31, no. 2, pp. 124–127.

HEFCE 2003. HEFCE website (online). Available at: www.hefce.ac.uk?News/HEFCE/2003/perfind.asp

Henderson, P. & Johnson, M. H. 2002. An innovative approach to developing the reflective skills of medical students. *BMC Medical Education*, vol. 2, no. 4, at www.biomedcetnral.com/1472–6920/2/4

Heschong, L. & Knecht, C. 2002. Daylighting makes a difference. *Educational Facility Planner*, vol. 37, no. 2, pp. 5–14.

Heschong Mahone Group 1999. *Daylighting in Schools: An Investigation Into the Relationship Between Daylighting and Human Performance*. San Francisco: Pacific Gas and Electric Company. Retrieved 3 July 2004 from: www.pge.com/003 _save_energy/003c_edu_train/pec/daylight/daylight.shtml

Higbee, K. L. 1996. *Your Memory: How It Works and How to Improve It*. New York: Marlowe and Company.

Higbee, K. L. 1997. Novices, apprentices and mnemonists: Acquiring expertise with the phonetic mnemonic. *Applied Cognitive Psychology*, vol. 11, pp. 147–161.

Hill, R. D., Allen, C. & McWhorter, P. 1991. Stories as a mnemonic aid for older learners. *Psychology and Aging*, vol. 6, no. 3, pp. 484–486.

Hoadley-Maidment, E. 1997. From 'story' to argument: The acquisition of essay writing skills in an open learning context. *Language and Education*, vol. 11, no. 1, pp. 55–68.

Holloway, J. 1999. Giving our students the time of day. *Educational Leadership*, vol. 57, no. 1, pp. 87–88. Retrieved 12 May 2004 from: www.ascd.org/publications/ed_lead/199909/holloway.html

Homa, D. 1983. An assessment of two extraordinary speed-readers. *Bulletin of the Psychonomic Society*, vol. 21, pp. 123–126.

Honey, P. & Mumford, A. 1982. *Manual of Learning Styles.* London: P. Honey.

Howe, E. R. 2004. Canadian and Japanese teachers' conceptions of critical thinking: A comparative study. *Teachers and Teaching*, vol. 10, no. 5, pp. 505–526.

Hron, A. & Friedrich, H. F. 2003. A review of web-based collaborative learning: Factors beyond technology. *Journal of Computer Assisted Learning*, vol. 19, pp. 70–79.

Huitt, W. 1988. Personality differences between Navajo and non-Indian college students: Implications for instruction. *Equity & Excellence*, vol. 24., no. 1, pp. 1, 71–74.

Imel, S. 1992. Reflective practice in adult education. *ERIC Digest*, no. 122. Retrieved 1 March 2006 from: www.ericdigests.org/1992-3/adult.htm.

Institute of Medicine 2004. *Dietary Reference Intakes for Water, Potassium, Sodium, Chloride, and Sulfate*, pp. 67–172. Washington, DC: National Academies Press. Retrieved online on 24 Feb. 05 from: www.iom.edu/report.asp?id=18495

Isen, A. M., Daubman, K. A. & Nowicki, G. B. 1987. Positive affect facilitates creative problem solving. *Journal of Personality and Social Psychology*, vol. 52, no. 6, pp. 1122–1131.

Jasper, M. A. 1999. Nurses' perceptions of the value of written reflection. *Nurse Education Today*, vol. 19, no. 6, pp. 452–463.

Jay, J. K. & Johnson, K. L. 2002. Capturing complexity: A typology of reflective practice for teacher education. *Teaching and Teacher Education*, vol. 10, no. 1, pp. 73–85.

Jensen, E. 2000. *Music and the Brain in Mind*. San Diego, CA: The Brain Store.

Johnson, R. T. & Johnson, D. W. 1994. An overview of co-operative learning. 'In J. Thousand, A. Villa & A. Nevin (eds), *Creativity and Collaborative Learning*. Baltimore: Brookes Press.

Just, M. A. & Carpenter, P. A. 1987. Speed Reading. In M. A. Just & P. A. Carpenter, *The Psychological of Reading and Language Comprehension*. Boston, MA: Allyn and Bacon, pp. 424–452.

Kaplan, E. J. & Keys, D. A. 1995. 'Teaching styles and learning styles: Which came first *Journal of Instructional Psychology*, vol. 22. pp. 29–33.

Kerka, S. 1996. Journal writing and adult learning. *ERIC Digest*, no. 174. Retrieved 1 March 2006 from: www.ericdigests.org/1997-2/journal.htm.

Khan, K. 2003. *Mnemonics for Medical Students*. London: Hodder Arnold.

Kiewra, K. A. & Frank, B. M. 1988. Encoding and external storage effects of personal lecture notes, skeletal notes, and detailed notes for field-independent and field-dependent learners. *Journal of Educational Research*, vol. 81, no. 3, pp. 143–148.

Klavas, A. 1994. In Greensboro, North Carolina, learning style program boosts achievement and test scores. *Clearing House*, vol. 67, no. 3, pp. 149–151.

Klemm, W. R. 1998. Eight ways to get students more engaged in online conferences. *T.H.E. Journal Online.* August 1998. www.thejournal.com/magazine/vault/A1997A.cfm

Kline, N. 1998. *Time to Think Listening to Ignite the Human Mind.* London: Cassell Illustrated.

Kolb, D. A. 1984. *Experience as the Source of Learning and Development.* Enplewood Cliffs, NJ: Prentice Hall.

Konstant, T. 2000. *Speed Reading.* Abingdon, Oxon: Hodder & Stoughton.

Koppenhaver, G. D. & Shrader, C. B. 2003. Structuring the classroom for performance: Cooperative learning with instructor-assigned teams. *Decision Sciences Journal of Innovative Education,* vol. 1, no. 1, pp. 1–22.

Kouzes, J. & Posner, B. 2003. *The Leadership Challenge.* San Francisco: Jossey Bass Wiley.

Kuller, R. & Lindsten, C. 1992. Health and behavior of children in classrooms with and without windows. *Journal of Environmental Psychology,* vol. 12, pp. 305–317.

Kunkel, J. G. & Shafer, W. E. 1997. Effects of student team learning in undergraduate auditing courses. *Journal of education for Business,* vol. 72, no. 4, pp. 197–200.

Kurfiss, J. G. 2000. *Critical Thinking: Theory, Research, Practice, and Possibilities.* San Francisco: Jossey Bass Wiley.

Lakoff, G. 1991. Metaphor in politics, an open letter to the Internet. philosophy. uoregon.edu/metaphor/lakoff–I.htm

Lakoff, G. & Johnson, M. 1980. *Metaphors We Live By.* Chicago: University of Chicago Press.

Langer, A. M. 2002. Reflecting on practice: Using learning journals in higher and continuing education. *Higher Education,* vol. 3, pp. 337–351.

Lawley, J. & Tompkins, P. 2000. *Metaphors in Mind: Transformation through Symbolic Modelling.* London: Developing Company Press.

Leung, D. Y. P. & Kember, D. 2003. The relationship between approaches to learning and reflection upon practice. *Educational Psychology,* vol. 23, no. 1, pp. 61–71.

Liebler, R. A. 2000. Assessing for Metacognition Competencies in an Adult Degree Completion Program. In K. Lee (ed.) *Access to Quality and Success: Applying Principles of Good Practice, AHEA 2000 Conference Proceedings.* Chicago: Adult Higher Education Alliance. Retrieved on 10 July 2004 from www.ahea.org/Assessing.htm

Lockyer, L., Patterson, J. & Harper, B. 2001. ICT in higher education: Evaluating outcomes for health education. *Journal of Computer Assisted Learning,* vol. 17, pp. 275–283.

Loo, R. 2002. The distribution of learning styles and types for hard and soft business majors. *Educational Psychology*, vol. 22, no. 3, pp. 349–360.

Lorch, R. F., Pugzles Lorch, E. & Klusewitz, M. A. 1993. College Students' Conditional Knowledge About Reading. *Journal of Education Psychology*, vol. 85, no. 2, pp. 239–252.

Lucas, B. 2001. *Power Up Your Mind: Learn Faster, Work Smarter.* London: Nicholas Brealey Publishing.

Luria, A. R. 1968. *The Mind of Mnemonist.* New York: Basic Books.

MacKenzie, K. R. 1997. Clinical application of group development ideas. *Group Dynamics: Theory, Research and Practice*, vol. 1, no. 4, pp. 275–287.

Magliano, J. P., Trabasso, T. & Graesser, A. C. 1999. Strategic processing during comprehension. *Journal of Educational Psychology*, vol. 91, no. 4, pp. 615–629.

Maguire, E. A., Gadrian, D. G., Johnsrude, I. S., Good, C. D., Ashburner, J., Frackowiak, R. S. T. & Frith, C. D. 2000. Navigation-related structural changes in the hippocampus of taxi drivers. *Proceedings of the National Academy of Sciences USA*, vol. 97, no. 8, pp. 4398–4403. Available at: www.pubmedcentral.gov/articlerender.fgci?tool=pubmed&pubmedid–10716738

Maier, J., Vaever Hartvig, N., Green, A. G. & Stodkilde-Jorgensen, H. 2004. Reading with the ears. *Neuroscience Letters*, vol. 364, no. 3, pp. 185–188.

Maloney, W. H. 2003. Connecting the texts of their lives to academic literacy: Creating success for at-risk first-year college students. *Journal of Adolescent & Adult Literacy*, vol. 46, no. 8, pp. 664–673.

Marshall Thomas, E. 1960. *The Harmless People.* Readers Union. Secker and Warburg.

Mason, R. 1991. Moderating educational computer conferencing. The Distance Education Online Symposium, *DEOSNEWS*, vol. 1. no. 19. Available online at: www.emoderators.com/papers/mason.html

Maudsley, G. & Strivens, J. 2000. Promoting professional knowledge, experiential learning and critical thinking for medical students. *Medical Education*, vol. 34, pp. 535–544.

Maylor, E. A. 1990. Age and Prospective Memory. *Quarterly Journal of Experimental Psychology*, vol. 42A, pp. 471–493.

McCutchen, D., Francis, M. & Kerr, S. 1997. Revising for meaning: Effects of knowledge and strategy. *Journal of Educational Psychology*, vol. 89, no. 4, pp. 667–676.

McDonald, B. & Boud, D. 2003. The impact of self-assessment on achievement: the effects of self assessment training on performance in external examinations. *Assessment in Education*, vol. 10, no. 2, pp. 210–220.

McFadzean, E. 1998. Enhancing creative thinking within organisations. *Management Decision*, vol. 36, no. 5, pp. 309–315.

McFadzean, E. & McKenzie, J. 2001. Facilitating virtual learning groups: A practical approach. *Journal of Management Development*, vol. 20, no. 6, pp. 470–494.

McGoun, E. G. 2003. Finance models as metaphor. *International Review of Financial Analysis*, vol. 12, pp. 421–433.

McGuire, S. & Edmondson, S. 2001. Student evaluation and assessment of group projects. *Journal of Geography in Higher Education*, vol. 25, no. 2, pp. 209–217.

McWhorter, K. T. 1998. *Academic reading*. New York: Longman.

Mednick, S., Nakayama, K. & Stickgold, R. 2003. Sleep-dependent learning: A nap is as good as a night. *Nature Neuroscience*, vol. 6, no. 7, pp. 697–8.

Meyer, B. J. F., Talbot, A. P. & Florencio, D. 1999. Reading rate and prose retrieval. *Scientific Studies of Reading*, vol. 3, Issue 4, pp. 303–330.

Meyer, B. J. F. & Poon, L. W. 2001. Effects of structure strategy training and signaling on recall of text. *Journal of Educational Psychology*, vol. 93, pp. 141–159.

Miller, D. A., Sadler, J. Z. & Mohl, P. C. 1993. Critical thinking in preclinical examinations. *Academic Medicine*, vol. 68, pp. 303–305.

Miller, G. A. 1956. The magical number seven, plus or minus two: Some limits on our capacity for processing information. *Psychological Review*, vol. 63, pp. 81–97. Retrieved 1 March 2006 from: http://cogprints.org/730/00/miller.html.

Miller, G. A. & Selfridge, J. A. 1950. Verbal context and the recall of meaningful material. *American Journal of Psychology*, vol. 63, pp. 76–185.

Mills, P. 2003. Group project work with undergraduate veterinary students. *Assessment and Evaluation in Higher Education*, vol. 28, no. 5, pp. 527–538.

Mokhtari, K. & Reichard, C. A. 2002. Assessing students' metacognitive awareness of reading strategies. *Journal of Educational Psychology*, vol. 94, no. 2, pp. 249–259.

Monaghan, P. & Shillcock, R. C. 2004. Hemispheric asymmetries in cognitive modelling: Connectionist modelling of unilateral visual neglect. *Psychological Review*, vol. 111, pp. 283–308.

Monaghan, P., Shillcock, R. C. & McDonald, S. 2004. Hemispheric asymmetries in the split-fovea model of semantic processing. *Brain and Language*, vol. 88, no. 3, pp. 339–354.

Moore, D. P. & Warner, E. 1998. *The Effect of Facilities on Student Achievement*. IssueTrak Briefing Papers, available online: www.cefpi.org/issue8.html

Moore, L. P. 1981. *Does This Mean My Kid's a Genius?* New York: McGraw-Hill.

Morrison, E. H., McLaughlin, C. & Rucker, L. 2002. Medical students' note-taking in a medical-biochemistry course: An initial exploration. *Medical Education*, vol. 36, pp. 384–386.

Morss, K. & Murray, R. 2001. Researching academic writing with a structured programme: Insights and outcomes. *Studies in Higher Education*, vol. 26, no. 1, pp. 35–52.

Muilenburg, M. A. & Zane, L. B. 2000. A framework for designing questions for online learning. *DEOSNEWS*, vol. 10, no. 2. (ISSN 1062–9416). Retrieved on 12 March 2006 from: www.emoderators.com/moderators/muilenburg.html

Mulligan, D. & Kirkpatrick, A. 2000. How much do they understand? Lectures, students and comprehension. *Higher Education Research and Development*, vol. 19, no. 3, pp. 311–335.

Nanda, B. R. 1985. *Ghandi and his Critics*. Dehli: Oxford University Press.

Nelson, B., Dunn, R., Griggs, S., Primavera, L., Fitzpatrick, M., Bacilious, Z. & Miller, R. 1993. Effects of learning style intervention on college students' retention and achievement. *Journal of College Student Development*, vol. 34, pp. 364–369.

Nelson, T. & McFadzean, E. 1998. Facilitating problem-solving groups: Facilitator competencies. *Leadership & Organization Development Journal*, vol. 19, no. 2, pp. 72–82.

Nestel, D. & Kidd, J. 2004. Teaching and learning about written communications in a United Kingdom medical school. *Education for Health*, vol. 17, no. 1, pp. 27–34.

Nganwa-Baqumah, M. & Mwamwenda, T. S. 1991. Effects on reading comprehension tests of matching and mismatching students' design preferences. *Perceptual and Motor Skills*, vol. 72, no. 3, pp. 947–951.

Norcini, J. F. 2003. Peer assessment of competence. *Medical Education*, vol. 37, pp. 539–543.

Norman, C. S., Rose, A. M. & Lehmann, C. M. 2004. Cooperative learning: Resources from the business disciplines. *Journal of Accounting Education*, vol. 22, pp. 1–28.

Norris, S. & Ennis, R. 1989. *Evaluating Critical Thinking*. Mawyah, NJ: Lawrence Erlbaum Associates.

Northedge, A. 1990. *The Good Study Guide*. Milton Keynes: Open University.

Norton, L. S., Tilley, A. J., Newstead, S. E. & Franklyn-Stokes, A. 2001. The pressure of assessment in undergraduate courses and their effect on student behaviours. *Assessment and Evaluation in Higher Education*, vol. 26, no. 3, pp. 269–284.

Novak, J. D. 1990. Concept mapping: A useful tool for science education. *Journal of Research in Science Teaching*, vol. 27, no. 10, pp. 937–949.

Oliver, R. & Omari, A. 2001. Student responses to collaborating and learning in a web-based environment. *Journal of Computer Assisted Learning*, vol. 17, pp. 34–47.

Orwell, G. 1970. *A Collection of Essays*. New York: Harcourt Publishers Ltd.

Page, S. & Meerabeau, L. 2000. Achieving change through reflective practice: Closing the loop. *Nurse Education Today*, vol. 20, no. 5, pp. 365–372.

Paris, S. G., Lipson, M. Y. & Wixson, K. K. 1983. Becoming a strategic reader. *Contemporary Educational Psychology*, vol. 8, pp. 293–316.

Parsons, L. M., Martinez, M. J., Delosh, E. L., Halpern, A. & Thaut, M. H. 2001. Musical and visual priming of visualization and mental rotation tasks. *Psychonomic Society Annual Abstracts*, November.

Pask, G. 1976. Styles and strategies of learning. *British Journal of Educational Psychology*, vol. 46, pp. 128–148.

Pask, G. 1988. Learning strategies, teaching strategies and conceptual or learning style. In R. Schmeck (ed.), *Perspectives on Individual Differences, Learning Strategies and Learning Styles*. New York & London: Plenum Press.

Paterson, B. L. 1995. Developing and maintaining reflection in clinical journals. *Nurse Education Today*, vol. 15, no., pp. 211–220.

Pauk, W. 2000. *How to Study in College*. 7th edn, Boston: Houghton Mifflin.

Paul, R. W. & Heaslip, P. 1995. Critical thinking and intuitive nursing practice. *Journal of Advanced Nursing*, vol. 22, pp. 40–47.

Peacock, M. 2001. Match or mismatch? Learning styles and teaching styles in EFL. *International Journal of Applied Linguistics*, vol. 11, no. 1, pp. 1–20.

Peters, M. 2000. Does constructivist epistemology have a place in nurse education? *Journal of Nursing Education*, vol. 39, no. 4, pp. 166–170.

Pike, G. R. 1997. Assessment measures: The California Critical Thinking Skills Test. *Assessment Update*, vol. 9, no. 2, pp. 10–11.

Pithers, R. T. & Soden, R. 2000. Critical thinking in education: A review. *Educational Research*, vol. 42, no. 3, pp. 273–249.

Prashnig, B. 1998. *The Power of Diversity*. Auckland, NZ: David Bateman Ltd.

Price, G. E., Dunn, R. & Dunn, K. 1991. *Productivity Environmental Preference Survey*. (PEPS Manual), Lawrence, KS: Price Systems, Inc. Website: www.learningstyle.com

Price, C. 2000. Self-directed learning in first year physiotherapy students: Reflections. In A. Herrmann & M. M. Kulski (eds), *Flexible Futures in Tertiary Teaching*. Proceedings of the 9th Annual Teaching Learning Forum 2–4 Feb 2000, Perth: Curtin University of Technology. Online at cea.curtin.edu.au/tlf/tlf2000/ price.html

Prichard, J. S. & Stanton, N. A. 1999. Testing Belbin's team role theory of effective groups, *Journal of Management Development*, vol. 18, no. 8, pp. 652–665.

Prior, J. 2000. Social psychology of a learning environment and the acquisition of critical thinking skills. *Social Work Education*, vol. 19, no. 5, pp. 501–511.

Pritchard, R. E., Romeo, G. C. & Muller, S. A. B. 1999. Integrating reading strategies into the accounting curriculum. *Authors College Student Journal*, vol. 33, no. 1, pp. 77–82.

Radford, T. 2003. Why is it so esay to raed wrods eevn wehn the lteetrs are mdduled up? *Guardian*, Thursday 25 September.

Railbert, M. 1996. Ethics and Computing, Living Responsibly in a Computerized World. In K. Bowyer, *Ethics and Computing: Living Responsibly in a Computerized*

World, pp. 409–413. © IEEE 1996. Retrieved online 14 Mar. 2005 from: www.udayton.edu/~richards/Miscellaneous%20essays/howtowrite.htm

Rauscher, F. H. 2002. Mozart and the mind: Factual and fictional effects of musical enrichment. In J. Aronson (ed.), *Improving Academic Achievement: Impact of Psychological Factors on Education*, pp. 267–278. New York: Academic Press.

Rauscher, F. H., Shaw, G., Levine, L. J., Ky, K. N. & Wright, E. L. 1993. Music and spatial task performance. *Nature*, vol. 365, p. 611.

Reed, M. & Mitchell, B. 2001. Using information technologies for collaborative learning in geography: A case study from Canada. *Journal of Geography in Higher Education*, vol. 25, no. 3, pp. 321–339.

Richard, J. T. 2003. Ideas on fostering creative problem in executive coaching. *Consulting Psychology Journal, Practice and Research*, vol. 55, no. 4, pp. 249–256.

Robson, J., Francis, B. & Read, B. 2002. Writes of passage: Stylistic features of male and female undergraduate history essays. *Journal of Further and Higher Education*, vol. 26, no. 4, pp. 351–362.

Ross, J., Drysdale, M. & Schulz, R. 2001. Cognitive learning styles and academic performance in two postsecondary computer application courses. *Journal of Research on Computing in Education*, vol. 33, no. 4, pp. 400–412.

Rowntree, D. 1995. The tutor's role in teaching via computer conferencing. *British Journal of Education Technology*, vol. 26, no. 3, pp. 205–215.

Rubin, D. C. & Wallace, W. T. 1989. Rhyme and reason: Analyses of dual retrieval cures. *Journal of Experimental Psychology: Learning, Memory and Cognition*, vol. 15, no. 4, pp. 698–709.

Ryan, A. 2003. Examination papers are set to produce no surprises. A student who has a reasonable memory ought to be able to get a Lowish 2.1 without much difficulty. *Times Higher Education Supplement*, 29 August, Issue 1604, p. 15.

Salmon, G. 2000. *E-moderating: The key to teaching on-line*. London: Kogan Page.

Salmon, G. 2002. *E-tivities: The key to active on-line learning*. London: Kogan Page.

Sandelands, E. 2000. Cyber tutoring and learning: How to facilitate learning online. At www.mcb.co.uk/imc/meetingplace/imc–seniortutors/71.html –

Schmidt, S. R. 1994. The effects of humor on sentence memory. *Journal of Experimental Psychology: Learning, Memory and Cognition*, vol. 20, no. 4, pp. 953–967.

Schnieder, M. 2002. Do school facilities affect academic outcomes? *National Clearing House for Educational Facilities*. Retrieved 11 May 2004 from: www.edfacilities.org/pubs/

Schon, D. 1983. *The Reflective Practitioner*. New York: Basic Books.

Seitz, J. A. 1989 (August). The development of bodily-kinesthetic intelligence: Implications for dance artistry. Paper presented at the American Psychological Association Convention, New Orleans, LA.

Seymour, B., Kinn, S. & Sutherland, N. 2003. Valuing both critical and creative thinking in clinical practice: narrowing the research-practice gap? *Journal of Advanced Nursing*, vol. 42, no. 3, pp. 288–296.

Sharp, J. E. 1998. Learning styles and technical communication: Improving communications and teamwork skills. Proceedings of the Frontiers in Education, 29th Annual Conference. Available at: engrng.pitt.edu/fie98/papers/1358.pdf

Sheard, A. G. & Kakabadse, A. P. 2002. From loose groups to effective teams: the nine key factors of the team landscape. *Journal of Management Development*, vol. 21, no. 2, pp. 133–151.

Shirey, L. L. & Reynolds, R. E. 1988. Effect of interest on attention and learning. *Journal of Educational Psychology*, vol. 80, no. 2, pp. 155–166.

Skelton, J. R., Wearn, A. M. & Hobbs, F. D. R. 2002. A concordance-based study of metaphoric expressions used by general practitioners and patients in consultation. *British Journal of General Practice*, vol. 52, no. 475, pp. 114–118.

Smith, K. & Tillema, H. 2001. Long term influences of portfolios on professional development. *Scandinavian Journal of Educational Research*, vol. 45, no. 2, pp. 183–202.

Smith, R. M. 1984. *Learning How to Learn*. Milton Keynes: Open University.

Steele, K. M., Brown, J. D. & Stoecker, J. A. 1999. Failure to confirm the Rauscher and Shaw description of recovery of the Mozart effect. *Perceptual and Motor Skills*, vol. 88, no. 3, pp. 843–848.

Stefani, L. 1994. Peer, self and tutor assessment: Relative reliabilities. *Studies in Higher Education*, vol. 19, no. 1, pp. 69–75.

Steinert, Y. 2004. Teaching methods – Student perceptions of effective small group teaching. *Medical Education*, vol. 38, no. 3, pp. 286–234.

Sternberg, J. J. 1997. *Thinking Styles.* Cambridge and New York: Cambridge University Press.

Stickgold, R., James, L. & Hobson, J. A. 2000. Visual discrimination learning requires sleep after training. *Nature Neuroscience*, vol. 3, pp. 1237–1238.

Stoerig, P. 1996. Varieties of vision: From blind responses to conscious recognition. *Trends in Neuroscience*, vol. 19, no. 9, pp. 401–406.

Sutherland, P., Badger, R. & White, G. 2002. How new students take notes at lectures. *Journal of Further and Higher Education*, vol. 26, no. 4, pp. 377–387.

Sweeney, D. 2000. Using MI profiles to optimize learning with graduate level studies. *MI News*, Winter 2000. Available online at: www.angelfire.com/oh/themidasnews/00win.html (accessed April 2003)

Talarico, J. M. & Rubin, D. C. 2003. Confidence, not consistency, characterizes flashbulb memories. *Psychological Science*, vol. 14, no. 5, pp. 455–461.

Taylor, B., Harris, L. A., Pearson, P. D. & Garcia, G. 1995. *Reading Difficulties.* New York: McGraw-Hill.

Terrell, S. & Dringus, L. 2000. An investigation of the effect of learning style on student success in an online learning environment. *Journal of Educational Technology Systems*, vol. 28, no. 3, pp. 231–238.

Terrell, S. 2002. Learning style as a predictor of success in a limited residency doctoral program. *The Internet in Higher Education*, vol. 5, no. 4, 345–352.

Terrell, S. 2005. Supporting different learning styles in an online learning environment: Does it really matter in the long run? *Online Journal of Distance Learning Administration*, vol. VIII, no. II, Summer. Retrieved 12 March 2006 from: www.westga.edu/~distance/ojdla/Summer82/terrell82.htm.

Thomas, E. M. 1989. *The Harmless People*. New York: Vintage.

Tiwari A., Avery, A. & Lai, P. 2003. Issues and innovations in nursing education: Critical thinking disposition on Hong Kong Chinese and Australian nursing students. *Journal of Advanced Nursing*, vol. 44, no. 3, pp. 298–307.

Torrance, M., Thomas, G. V. & Robinson, E. J. 2000. Individual differences in undergraduate essay-writing strategies: A longitudinal study. *Higher Education*, vol. 39, pp. 181–200.

Tuckman, B. W. 1965. Developmental sequences in small groups. *Psychological Bulletin*, vol. 63, no. 6, pp. 384–399.

Tuckman, B. W. & Jensen, M. 1977. Stages of small group development revisited. *Group & Organization Studies*, vol. 2, pp. 419–427.

Tulving, E. 1967. The effects of presentation and recall of information in free-recall learning. *Journal of Verbal Learning and Behaviour*, vol. 6, pp. 175–184.

United States Department of Education 2000. Impact of inadequate school facilities on student learning. Retrieved 08 May 2004 from: www.ed.gov/offices/OESE/archives/inits/construction/impact2.html

Van Dongen, H. P., Maislin, G., Mullington, J. M. & Dinges, D. F. 2003. The cumulative cost of additional wakefulness: Dose-response effects on neurobehavioral functions and sleep physiology from chronic sleep restriction and total sleep deprivation. *Sleep*, vol. 26, no. 2, pp. 117–126.

Verhaeghen, P., Marcoen, A. & Goossens, L. 1992. Improving memory performance in the the aged through Mnemonic Training: A meta-analytic study. *Psychology and Aging*, vol. 7, no. 2, pp. 241–251.

Wagner, U., Gais, S., Haider, H., Verleger, R. & Born, J. 2004. Sleep inspires insight. *Nature*, vol. 427, no. 6972, pp. 352–355.

Wallace, J. 1995. When teachers' learning styles differ from those of their students. *Journal of Instructional Psychology*, vol. 22, pp. 99–100.

Walsh, C. M. & Hardy, R. C. 1999. Dispositional differences in critical thinking related to gender and academic major. *Journal of Nursing Education*, vol. 38, no. 4, pp. 149–155.

Watson, G. & Glaser, E. M. 1952. *Watson-Glaser Critical Thinking Appraisal Manual*. Orlando, FL: Harcourt Brace Jovanovich.

Wheary, J. & Ennis, R. H. 1995. Gender bias in critical thinking: Continuing the dialogue. *Educational Theory*, Spring, on-line at: www.ed.uiuc.edu/EPS/Educational-theory/contents/45_2_Wheary_Ennis.asp

Wheelan, S. 2003. An initial exploration of the internal dynamics of leadership teams. *Consulting Psychology Journal, Practice and Research*, vol. 55, no. 3, pp. 179–188.

Wilson, T. L. & Brown, T. L. 1997. Reexamination of the effect of Mozart's music on spatial-task performance. *Journal of Psychology*, vol. 131, pp. 365–370.

Winograd, P. & Johnson, P. 1987. Some considerations for advancing the teaching of reading comprehension. *Education Psychologist*, vol. 22, pp. 213–230.

Withnall, A. 2001. Understanding learning styles of older workers. *Adults Learning*, vol. 13, no. 3, pp. 17–20.

Wolfson, A. 1999. Sleeping in: Changing high school start times improves performance. *Advance Respiratory Care*, vol. 8, no. 8, pp. 14–16.

Wu, J. H. & Yuan, Y. 2003. Improving searching and reading performance: The effect of highlighting and text color coding. *Information & Management*, vol. 40, no. 7, pp. 617–637.

Wyon, D. P., Andersen, I. B. & Lundqvist, G. R. 1979. The effects of moderate heat stress on mental performance. *Scandinavian Journal of Work, Environment, and Health*, vol. 5, pp. 352–361.

Yan, L. & Kember, D. 2004. Avoider and engager approaches by out-of-class groups: The group equivalent to individual learning approaches. *Learning and Instruction*, vol. 14, pp. 27–49.

Yeh, L. M. & Chen, H. H. 2003. Comparison affective dispositions toward critical thinking across Chinese and American baccalaureate nursing students. *Journal of Nursing Research*, vol. 11, no. 1, pp. 39–46.

Yong, F. L. & McIntyre, J. D. 1992. A comparative study of the learning styles preferences of students with learning disabilities and students who are gifted. *Journal of Learning Disabilities*, vol. 25, no. 2, pp. 124–132.

Zinsser, W. 2001. *On Writing Well: The Classic Guide to Writing Nonfiction*. New York: Harper Resource.

Index